The Kentucky Bicentennial Bookshelf
Sponsored by

KENTUCKY HISTORICAL EVENTS CELEBRATION COMMISSION

KENTUCKY FEDERATION OF WOMEN'S CLUBS

and Contributing Sponsors

AMERICAN FEDERAL SAVINGS & LOAN ASSOCIATION

ARMCO STEEL CORPORATION, ASHLAND WORKS

A. ARNOLD & SON TRANSFER & STORAGE CO., INC. / ASHLAND OIL, INC.

BAILEY MINING COMPANY, BYPRO, KENTUCKY / BEGLEY DRUG COMPANY

J. WINSTON COLEMAN, JR. / CONVENIENT INDUSTRIES OF AMERICA, INC.

IN MEMORY OF MR. AND MRS. J. SHERMAN COOPER BY THEIR CHILDREN

CORNING GLASS WORKS FOUNDATION / MRS. CLORA CORRELL

THE COURIER-JOURNAL AND THE LOUISVILLE TIMES

COVINGTON TRUST & BANKING COMPANY

MR. AND MRS. GEORGE P. CROUNSE / GEORGE E. EVANS, JR.

FARMERS BANK & CAPITAL TRUST COMPANY / FISHER-PRICE TOYS, MURRAY

MARY PAULINE FOX, M.D., IN HONOR OF CHLOE GIFFORD

MARY A. HALL, M.D., IN HONOR OF PAT LEE,

JANICE HALL & MARY ANN FAULKNER

OSCAR HORNSBY INC. / OFFICE PRODUCTS DIVISION IBM CORPORATION

JERRY'S RESTAURANTS / ROBERT B. JEWELL

LEE S. JONES / KENTUCKIANA GIRL SCOUT COUNCIL

KENTUCKY BANKERS ASSOCIATION / KENTUCKY COAL ASSOCIATION, INC.

THE KENTUCKY JOCKEY CLUB, INC. / THE LEXINGTON WOMAN'S CLUB

LINCOLN INCOME LIFE INSURANCE COMPANY

LORILLARD A DIVISION OF LOEW'S THEATRES, INC.

METROPOLITAN WOMAN'S CLUB OF LEXINGTON / BETTY HAGGIN MOLLOY

MUTUAL FEDERAL SAVINGS & LOAN ASSOCIATION

NATIONAL INDUSTRIES, INC. / RAND MCNALLY & COMPANY

PHILIP MORRIS, INCORPORATED / MRS. VICTOR SAMS

SHELL OIL COMPANY, LOUISVILLE

SOUTH CENTRAL BELL TELEPHONE COMPANY

SOUTHERN BELLE DAIRY CO. INC.

STANDARD OIL COMPANY (KENTUCKY)

STANDARD PRINTING CO., H. M. KESSLER, PRESIDENT

STATE BANK & TRUST COMPANY, RICHMOND

THOMAS INDUSTRIES INC. / TIP TOP COAL CO., INC.

MARY L. WISS, M.D. / YOUNGER WOMAN'S CLUB OF ST. MATTHEWS

The Harvest
and
The Reapers

Oral Traditions of Kentucky

KENNETH and MARY CLARKE

THE UNIVERSITY PRESS OF KENTUCKY

Research for The Kentucky Bicentennial Bookshelf
is assisted by a grant from the
National Endowment for the Humanities.
Views expressed in the Bookshelf do not
necessarily represent those of the Endowment.

ISBN: 0-8131-0201-4
Library of Congress Catalog Card Number: 74-7872

A statewide cooperative scholarly publishing agency
serving Berea College, Centre College of Kentucky,
Eastern Kentucky University, Georgetown College,
Kentucky Historical Society, Kentucky State University,
Morehead State University, Murray State University,
Northern Kentucky State College, Transylvania University,
University of Kentucky, University of Louisville, and
Western Kentucky University.
Editorial and Sales Offices: Lexington, Kentucky 40506

To the memory of a great humanist
DR. GORDON WILSON, SR.

Contents

Preface

JOURNALISTS, performers, authors, and political orators have dispensed Kentucky folklore for decades. Kentuckians have many volumes of songbooks and folktales drawn from two hundred years of unique regional folklife. Kentucky historians have stressed the role of the folkways of their frontier people.

The story that has not been told is about the men and women who have devoted their energies to the collection and study of folklore. Many of these are Kentucky scholars seeking to fill in gaps of knowledge about language, literature, music, history, and sociology. Others are devoted amateurs, and still others are performing artists. All have contributed in various ways to an understanding of the nature and role of oral tradition in Kentucky.

A brief survey of the chronology and some of the personalities associated with that understanding is presented here. To all those people not mentioned in these pages—students, informants, singers, tale-tellers—who have contributed to the pages of the *Kentucky Folklore Record* and who have helped in other ways, a debt of gratitude is hereby acknowledged.

1

INTRODUCTION

The technical song catcher who goes into the mountains to find only versions of those songs which are listed in the famous Child Collection is about as thorough as the man who wishes to study the peculiar impressions made by pigs' feet in a country lane by studying only the tracks of red pigs.

THOMAS D. CLARK, *The Kentucky*

KENTUCKIANS throughout their history have developed a self-image shaped and sustained by a love of tradition. The intertwining expressions *of* Kentuckians and *about* Kentuckians reinforce each other. Things people have said and written about the Commonwealth and its people have created a reputation for them to live up to, a reputation for high-spirited living and romantic anachronisms, at times implying mysterious and forbidden doings as well as broad humor and adventurous action. Kentuckians expressing themselves in song and story, and even in everyday speech, have established their image for the nation at large. Actually, it is not a single image; it is a composite, a montage of bluegrass and bourbon, mountains and marksmen, song and story. It began even before there was a set of boundaries, when people were uncertain about how to spell "Kentucky."

However it was spelled, the word designated a wild and wonderful place beyond mountains and rivers, a place without constraints or history. Folklore about Kentucky and men daring enough to go there must have had its beginnings in some obscure, unrecorded conversations, reports two or three times removed from their origins about exploits of the Long Hunters with bears, buffalo, and Indians, exaggerated here and there for the sake of a good telling.

Unfortunately, no folktale collector was lurking in the taverns or shops to record such tales, but indirect evidence suggests that typical tall tales about game and wonders of the natural world filtered out of the Kentucky wilderness even before permanent settlers began filtering in, for the earliest written records which reflect the reputation of the place and its people show that Kentucky folklore had already taken firm root.

In *The Frontier Mind*, Arthur K. Moore sums up what he calls "the garden archetype," exaggerated popular beliefs about Kentucky which contributed to the first rush of settlers seeking a kind of Eden. For a time, he writes,

The Garden of the West sustained the illusion, and that interval was sufficient to permit faith and emotion to congeal, with the result that the Kentucky myth entered the cultural stream as a hardy organism, proof against fact and reason. The American imagination seized upon the short period when the forest was indeed majestic and the tenant heroic, and wove the golden threads into a superlative tapestry which, like good whiskey, improves with age.

The popular image of Kentucky persists. In the 1960s, a college professor picked up two young hitchhikers as he drove to visit relatives in Carter County. In the ensuing conversation he discovered that his passengers were college students from Oregon. Carrying a tape recorder, they had hitchhiked from Oregon to eastern Kentucky to

2

collect folksongs. Neither of the students had visited the area before. Neither had any leads, yet they were supremely confident that they could, in spite of ignorance and inexperience, collect folksongs in eastern Kentucky.

The students were acting on some of the folklore about Kentuckians. They "knew," just as "everyone knows," that people in the mountains of Kentucky sit out on front porches, pick banjos or pluck mountain dulcimers, and sing ancient ballads in a pure (or maybe just nearly pure) Elizabethan dialect. The professor was amused and appalled.

The proper moral for such a story should have the young men end their quest in disappointment, a little wiser about collecting folksongs and a little better informed about contemporary Kentucky. However, since this is a true story, it must go its own way to its inappropriate ending. The kindly professor just happened to have some singing relatives. He drove the blundering boys to a singer and made it possible for them to record some traditional songs.

The story ends there. Did the students, fired with enthusiasm derived from their first easy success, go on to record other singers? Did they return to Oregon loaded with tape recordings of songs bagged in Kentucky—just as the Long Hunters returned to their homes loaded with pelts from the wilderness? And did they swagger and brag about their Appalachian adventures, stretching the truth a little to make a good yarn? And if they did, was their telling of a good story another contribution to the folklore about Kentucky?

Other examples come to mind. Almost two centuries before the Oregon students blundered across the nation to collect Kentucky folksongs, John Filson depended on the veracity of Daniel Boone for some aspects of Kentucky history. Boone, from all accounts we can assemble, was a fabulous woodsman. Hunters, fishermen, and explorers have been known to make a good story a little better. Is it possible that John Filson, ostensibly a historian, was unknowingly acting the role of folklorist as he recorded tall tales from Kentucky?

When Samuel Woodworth wrote "The Hunters of Kentucky" in 1822, he had in mind the Kentucky riflemen who helped achieve victory against the British in New Orleans on January 8, 1815. The presence of Kentucky marksmen at that battle is historical fact, but the lines of the song suggest supra-fact—the stuff of folklore.

> For 't is not often that you see
> A hunter from Kentucky.
> Oh! Kentucky, the hunters of Kentucky,
> The hunters of Kentucky.

This was not a folksong when the composer wrote it, but field collection has proved its later adoption into oral tradition. The song illustrates part of the theme presented here: folklore engenders popular literature which enhances the folklore which inspires the writer. . . . It becomes a cyclic phenomenon, changing and refining the image as time passes, and, like a perpetual-motion machine, providing its own energy. The idiom of the people continues to project a popular image which becomes a part of the folklore, not only of Kentucky but also of the nation.

Too frequently the would-be collector of folklore sets out to demonstrate his preconceived opinion of what the folklore is, and, failing to find what he wants, assumes that there is none or that it has eluded him. Or, because his fixed idea of what he wants narrows his aim, he collects only the material that suits his conception, thereby supporting his preconceived opinion, even if it is not very supportable. The results of that kind of collection have helped create a kind of folklore about the folklore of Kentucky!

It is barely possible that a modern collector could find

an ancient granny sitting in a chimney corner, sucking on her pipe and telling long European-style folktales in a language larded with quaint archaisms, but such a discovery today would not demonstrate anything valid about contemporary Kentucky folklore. It would be a curiosity only, like encountering a live mountain lion in Appalachia.

It is also barely possible that a modern collector could find a barefoot maid weeding the garden and singing "Barbara Allan" from pure, uncorrupted oral tradition, but that discovery too would be a curiosity, out of place and out of time. Most maids, barefoot or shod, go to high school, watch television, and listen to stereo phonograph records. If they happen to sing "Barbara Allan" they are likely to be singing in imitation of a rather pleasant recorded rendition by Joan Baez, a professional singer. It is true that granny may say "That's not the way I heard it," but granny, too, listens to television.

Kentucky is a modern state, a state which, by official 1970 census figures, is now classified as urban. Kentucky is rich in folklore, part of which has been expressed by tale-telling grannies and ballad-singing maids. But times change. To think of contemporary Kentucky folklore in terms of oral traditions perpetuating Scottish ballads and English Jack tales would be analogous to thinking of Kentucky agriculture in terms of performance by yoked oxen.

What, then, is a realistic presentation of Kentucky oral traditions? As presented here, it is the idiom of the people expressing attitudes in beliefs, legends, anecdotes, and songs. The expressions have been conditioned by settlement patterns—who settled, where they settled, and where they came from—and by the unique chronicle of events which have affected those people during the history of the state. The idiom of the people projects into festivals, processions, ceremonies, and literature, all of which reflect an awareness that many strands of tradition are woven into the fabric of Kentuckiana.

The institution of the Kentucky colonel is as much rooted in the folk image as is the institution of rural gospel singing. And just as the institution of the Kentucky colonel is shrewdly exploited by the commercial vendors of fried chicken, so the gospel singing is shrewdly exploited by the phonograph recording industry. These examples serve to remind one of the commercial vendors of mint juleps at Churchill Downs on Derby Day, with associations reaching out to Kentucky bourbon, Kentucky thoroughbreds, and Kentucky bluegrass. Indeed, there is no way to separate the strands. The granny in the chimney corner, though a past institution as an individual, lives on as a part of the time-depth fabric of Kentucky folklore, for folklore by its very definition is a montage of time-honored skills, not the least of which is oral expression. Those mellowed skills, reaching back beyond the boundaries and history of Kentucky, alter their expression and impact with the accretion of each new generation's experience.

If one seeks quaint old European ballads and tales in modern Kentucky, he may feel that the oral traditions of the commonwealth have been sadly depleted. If, however, he seeks a lively revival of interest in traditional skills and expressions, he will be impressed by its role in contemporary culture. If he wants to verify the popular impression that Kentucky retains richly regional speech characteristics, he will find recently compiled evidence to support that impression. In fact, verification of the true nature and extent of all aspects of Kentucky folklore is gradually becoming a simple matter of consulting recorded facts rather than depending on impressionistic conjecture, for the facts have been accumulating at a steadily accelerating pace for more than a half-century.

In 1912 a group of interested Kentucky citizens, both scholars and laymen, established the Kentucky Folklore Society. In those earliest years, some collected Kentucky folklore was being published in the *Journal of*

American Folklore. Though the Kentucky Folklore Society circulated some early newsletters and several volumes of *Kentucky Folk-Lore and Poetry* magazine during the 1920s and 1930s, publication was sporadic until 1955, when the *Kentucky Folklore Record,* a quarterly publication of the Society, was founded. The *Kentucky Folklore Record* is widely circulated to university and public libraries in the United States and to some of the principal folklore centers abroad. It has contained, by report or by direct contribution, samples of the work of practically every investigator of Kentucky folklore. "Samples" is a carefully chosen word, for some investigators have collected extensively, publishing occasionally in various media but preserving much of their work in unpublished archives. The bulk of archive material is available for study, however, making it possible for the truly inquiring modern searcher to develop an accurate impression of Kentucky folklore, past and present.

Much of what follows has been drawn from the pages of the *Kentucky Folklore Record* and the Western Kentucky University Folklore and Folklife Collection.

2

FOLK IMAGES OF KENTUCKY

THE FARTHER BACK one traces the precise nature of folklore in and about Kentucky, the more one must rely on fragments of texts and allusions such as the one to the hunters of Kentucky cited above. Verification of a growing Kentucky mystique throughout the nineteenth century depends on the literature of the period. Much of that literature is "fugitive" or "sub-literary," ephemeral sketches and fictions which appeared in newspapers or even less substantial outlets. Such materials were often anonymous or credited to a pseudonym. They suggest a body of popular lore which provided the raw material for some of the established writers of the century.

Notwithstanding some late nineteenth-century beginnings, notably the founding of the American Folklore Society in 1888, until the early years of the twentieth century there was no systematic effort to collect folklore anywhere in the United States. Not until mid-century was there a sufficient body of scholarship, academic training, methodology, and technical equipment (such as the tape recorder) to permit wide-scale field collecting, archiving, and analysis of the whole range of folklore. Kentucky, like the rest of the union, contributed richly to the nation's stock of folklore, but public knowledge of the material was acquired by indirection, from the transformations wrought by the pens of journalists and creative writers.

Bret Harte's "Luck of Roaring Camp" is illustrative. An important character in the story is Kentuck, whose groping finger the newborn Luck has grasped. Kentuck has a rough exterior but his essential kindness surfaces:

> "How goes it?" said Kentuck, looking past Stumpy toward the candle-box. "All serene," replied Stumpy. "Anything up?" "Nothing." There was a pause—an embarrassing one— Stumpy still holding the door. Then Kentuck had recourse to his finger, which he held up to Stumpy. "Rastled with it,—the d—d little cuss," he said, and retired.

Harte gives Kentuck center stage in the closing paragraph of the story:

> It needed but a glance to show them Kentuck lying there, cruelly crushed and bruised, but still holding the Luck of Roaring Camp in his arms. As they bent over the strangely assorted pair, they saw that the child was cold and pulseless. "He is dead," said one. Kentuck opened his eyes. "Dead?" he repeated feebly. "Yes, my man, and you are dying too." A smile lit the eyes of the expiring Kentuck.

Harte's sentimental presentation of a Kentuckian in the California goldfields contributed a romantic variant of an image already well established. Much earlier, Colonel Nimrod Wildfire, stage hero of James Kirke Paulding's *The Lion of the West* (1831), was characterized as a "raw Kentuckian" of the type described by John James Audubon—marksmen who had both their living and pleasure from their remarkably effective long rifles. In a long "ring-tailed roarer" speech the character in the play closes by saying, "My name is Nimrod Wildfire— half horse, half alligator and a touch of airthquake— that's got the prettiest sister, fastest horse and ugliest dog in the District, and can outrun, outjump, throw down, drag out and whip any man in all Kaintuck."

9

Many writers of the nineteenth century drew upon the general idea of the "raw Kentuckian" as a bold frontier type, colorfully verbose and aggressive. The image originated in real life, but the playback in literature fixed it permanently in the national consciousness.

John Q. Anderson, writing about popular humor of the Old South in *With the Bark On* (1967), and drawing many examples from old newspaper files, remarks on "Salt River roaring" associated with the men who built rafts and flatboats to float down the Mississippi River to New Orleans. Because so many of the raftsmen and boatmen came from Kentucky, river men of their kind, regardless of origin, came to be called "Kaintucks."

The lean, shrewd backwoodsman epitomized in the name "Kaintuck" is, of course, only one portion of the composite folk image of Kentucky and Kentuckians. The alliterative triad, Bluegrass, Belles, and Bourbon, refers to other important elements. Bluegrass suggests the gracious life of the Old South, ample pastures, high-bred horses, and an aristocracy which blends well with the "Kentucky colonel" tradition. It would appear that Kentuckians have always boasted about the beauty of Kentucky women. Regardless of what the objective facts may be (if one can be objective about beauty!), the boast is comfortably at home with the connotations of aristocratic chivalry.

Kentucky bourbon traditions reach in two directions. On the one hand, bourbon is at home with gracious living, with the julep, which itself has come to be so closely associated with the Derby at Churchill Downs that it may be the principal symbol of that great sports occasion. On the other hand, bourbon, sometimes claimed as a Kentucky discovery, suggests the still, which suggests the moonshiner, which suggests the hillman, the revenuer, and all the rest of that persistent complex, an important element of which is the feud.

Some of the darker aspects of Kentucky tradition could be depressing to Kentuckians if it were not for a fabulously saving sense of humor. Many Kentuckians long ago began taking some delight in referring to themselves as hillbillies in an engaging willingness to capitalize on general folklore about the state. The self-confessed hillbilly could be an urban professional person, or he could just as easily be the authentic item. It is good-natured as long as the Kentuckian rather than the outsider initiates the identification.

With the spoofing proliferation of Kentucky Colonel commissions, recipients gravely frame them and hang them up alongside diplomas and other memorabilia. One can be sure that the anonymous wag who composed this toast was a Kentuckian:

> *Here's to Old Kentucky,*
> *The State where I was born,*
> *Where the corn is full of kernels,*
> *And the Colonels full of "corn."*

Josiah H. Combs was one of the scholars who gave early impetus and direction to the Kentucky Folklore Society. Born and bred a Kentucky hillman, Combs contributed to the cluster of ironies in the history of serious folklore study by going to France to study for his doctorate. His published dissertation, an important contribution to the study of Southern folksong in the United States, was necessarily in French, *Folk-Songs du Midi des États-Unis* (1925).

Combs's completion of a doctorate at the University of Paris marked the culmination of an educational odyssey which began at Hindman Settlement School and progressed to Transylvania University. His education was interrupted several times, principally by various school-teaching jobs and by World War I. In 1915 he edited an anthology of Kentucky materials, principally poetry, under the title *All That's Kentucky.*

The anthology is a strangely mixed selection of materials which range from the outrageously sentimental to the parody, from weak imitations of the most cloying romanticism to realistic vignettes. Throughout, the collection shines with what must have been Josiah Combs's puckish sense of humor as he arranged selections of jarringly opposite tone and content back to back.

This 1915 anthology may not be *all* that's Kentucky, but, accumulating as it does materials reaching back into the nineteenth century, it reveals an easygoing objectivity about the maturing traditions making up the Kentucky montage. Combs displays his folkloristic instinct for ferreting out the images of Kentucky and Kentuckians by briefly quoting Europeans who showed their awareness of those images in their writings: Scott in "Marmion"; Byron in *Don Juan;* Tennyson in "On Sublimity"; and Wells in "The Passionate Friends."

Unvarnished praise of Kentucky appears in Captain Jack Harding's "Kentucky":

> *Loved Kentucky, land of the blest,*
> *Never by the heel of tyrant oppressed;*
> *Plenty pours from the horn of Cornucopia,*
> *Happy are the children of the land of Utopia.*

But the anonymous writer who penned "The Kentucky Mountaineer" responded with another view:

> *Man born in the wilds of Kentucky is of feud days,*
> *   and full of virus.*
> *He fisheth, fiddleth, fusseth and fighteth all the*
> *   days of his busy life.*

H. J. Lunger, whose "The Kentucky Colonel" first appeared in *The Transylvanian,* added to the series of good-natured jests by poking fun at both the institution and the spelling of colonel:

> *A night-riding colonel*
> *From babyhood volonel,*
> *With hoodlums fratolonel.*

Whether the writers were serious or satirical, an appreciative sense of history runs deeply throughout the volume. Colonel William Lightfoot Visscher, as his name might suggest, reflects the aristocratic bluegrass aspects of Kentucky tradition:

From the days of Boone and Kenton,
In the "Dark and Bloody Ground,"
To the days when homes and gardens
In the bluegrass land abound;
Since it sent its leaden messengers
To bring the savage down,
We have blest the good old rifle
Of Kentucky and renown.

Though Colonel Visscher's historic Kentucky rifle hangs in the hall as a reminder of the nobler aspects of Kentucky history, James Foley, Jr., in "Feud Time in Kentucky," sees the rifle as a continuing symbol of the mountain man's activities:

When the dew is on the mountain
And the corn is in the still—
When the feudist stalks the feudist
Through the valley, o'er the hill—

Finally, James Tandy Ellis's "Ten Broek" is a reminder of the racing tradition—one which runs strong from the earliest settlement of the commonwealth, one which may outlast most of the others. The poem is about a great match race between Ten Broek and Molly. The race has special significance for folklorists in that it spawned a native American ballad. The poem and the ballad have no similarity other than the fact that they deal with the same race. This is part of Ellis's description:

Yes, I saw that four-mile run
Down at Louisville in July,

13

Hot?—it seemed the brilin' sun
Flamed the clouds along the sky.
Ten Broek, white with lathered foam
Like an eagle cut the air,
Brought his colors safely home,
Writ his name in history there.

With the single exception of an allusion to a native American ballad, all the references above are literary. The relationship of these materials to a discussion of Kentucky folklore requires further explanation.

The idea that the flowering of the art forms of a people springs from the roots of folk expression traces back to the German philosopher-folklorist Johann Gottfried von Herder (1744–1803). Simply stated, the idea is that the basic vehicle—the language—is not the creation of the elite or intellectual classes. It is, rather, the creation and common property of the folk. Although the artist may manipulate language creatively, the vehicle he manipulates is not of his making. The basic shaping force of a national or regional literature, then, is the voice of the anonymous people.

American scholars have developed this thought as it applies to American literature, most notably perhaps in the writings of Constance Rourke (*American Humor: A Study of the National Character*, 1931).

In the life and works of Josiah Combs one sees a paradigm of the Herder-Rourke thesis. Combs was a Kentucky mountain boy, bright enough to be drawn into the influence of the Hindman Settlement School. He sang Kentucky mountain ballads and played the mountain dulcimer. At the settlement school, his teacher, Miss Katherine Pettit, found his traditional songs interesting enough to send a few transcriptions to the editor of the *Journal of American Folklore*, where the texts were published in 1907.

The distinguished Harvard scholar G. L. Kittredge, who edited the songs for the journal, wrote an introduction: "The following ballads and rhymes from the mountains of Kentucky were collected recently by Miss Katherine Pettit of Hindman, Knott County, in that State. Miss Pettit has had the kindness to send the material to the Journal for publication." Kittredge gallantly mentioned the name of the contributor, then got down to business: a presentation of the texts in verse form (no music), following the general procedure already established at Harvard by Francis Child. The texts and some comparative notes were the focus of attention— not the singer, not the music, not the community or family tradition. This small collection, among the earliest published texts of Kentucky folksong, shows how faltering was the beginning of Kentucky collection and study.

At Transylvania University, Josiah Combs happily came under the influence of Professor Hubert Shearin, another pioneer member of the Kentucky Folklore Society. Together, Shearin and Combs published *A Syllabus of Kentucky Folksongs* in 1911. Combs also found that he could get appreciative audiences for his lecture tours and folksong recitals. By the time of his doctoral dissertation at the University of Paris in 1925, the Kentucky mountain boy was both a seasoned scholar and a seasoned performer. During his academic career he produced learned books and articles ranging over literature, language, and folklore.

The emphasis here on the anthology of Kentucky poetry is appropriate. Josiah Combs was a literary scholar. About 90 percent of all collection and study of folklore has taken the literary approach. In spite of some recent shift to certain aspects of material culture, such as architecture and arts and crafts, folklore is still thought of primarily as the verbal expressions of ordinary people— a kind of unwritten literature, both spoken and sung. Josiah Combs, with his mountain origin and broad interests in literature and language, could study regional dialect, folksong, folktale, poetry, and elite literature without any sense of conflict, for these are all parts of a great spectrum of human expression which has no inherent partitioning.

Just as Josiah Combs progressed from his folk origins to international recognition, so folklore reaches up and branches out from its humble origins into all levels of culture and expression. And just as the products of language (poem, novel, song) cannot be separated from their linguistic vehicle, so the popular image of a culture cannot be separated from the reiterated and recombined folk expressions that first gave it form.

3

KENTUCKY WORDS
AND BRIEF EXPRESSIONS

IN 1972 a folklorist driving along a country road in Edmonson County stopped to ask directions. He was trying
to find an elderly farmer reputed to be an expert wielder
of a broadax. A sturdy middle-aged resident responded
enthusiastically to the inquiry, observing that the man
who could use the broadax was his uncle. He went on to
describe the older man's skills. "He's a glib old man,"
he said. "He can do almost anything with his hands."

The folklorist made a mental note of the word "glib"
associated with handskills. It was something to check in
the dictionaries. His subsequent verification that "glib"
once denoted a wider range of meaning than shallowness in speech was gratifying; he had tallied one
more example of archaic speech in a modern setting.

Word-watching can become as great a hobby as birdwatching. Indeed, both activities, each requiring a special kind of observation, can appeal to the same field
worker. When he is not finding one, he may find the
other, or in pursuit of one, he may get a bonus by happening upon the other.

If folklore is considered to be primarily verbal expression, then the simple word is a good place to begin
collecting. Speech is a creation of the anonymous folk,

everywhere different according to the cumulative heritage of the region. There is not one Kentucky dialect; there are many. Pennyrile speech differs from Bluegrass speech just as Appalachian mountain speech differs from Purchase speech. To the carefully trained ear, Logan County pronunciation differs from Warren County pronunciation even though the distance separating the homes of the speakers is less than the distance between widely separated suburbs of Louisville.

What is ordinarily called folk speech is the unaffected speech of ordinary people untutored in niceties of oration or elocution. Elements of folk speech that delight the word hunter are special regional pronunciations and vocabulary items signifying the strong thrust of tradition.

"I holp him yesterday," pronounced in such a way that holp sounds more like hope and yesterday sounds more like yistiddy, is an example of unaffected speech easy to come by in many parts of rural Kentucky. The speaker says "I holp him yesterday" instead of "I helped him yesterday" because he has grown up with surviving fragments of an Old English (or Anglo-Saxon) conjugation. Before the Norman conquest, an English speaker used the full conjugation of the verb, including these forms: hulpe, hulpen, and holpen. Traditional Kentucky speech is richly laced with similar anachronistic elements, often embedded in expressions like ballads, folktales, riddles and proverbs, where the context is an aid in their preservation. Although the collector of songs and tales will inevitably encounter interesting speech items, not every collector makes a point of recording them.

One rural Kentuckian who regularly uses the "I holp him" form has become self-conscious about holp since he discovered its antiquity. He now regularly corrects this by using the past tense hepped when he is talking to "educated" people, happily unaware that his verb is still an example of regional dialect.

Apparently the speech habits of "Kaintucks" were singular enough to attract attention early in the history of the Commonwealth, and journalistic writers capitalized on this aspect of the image of the "raw" frontiersman. Exaggeration of dialect for humorous purposes is one more illustration of how a folklore *about* Kentucky folklore could develop. The speech of Kentucky mountaineers, for example, has been described as "pure Anglo-Saxon." Actually, there never has been a "pure" Anglo-Saxon speech, even in England before the Norman conquest. The Anglo-Saxon myth has been promoted, however, enough to create the joke about the native who boasted that his people spoke "Angry-Saxon."

An even stronger popular belief about speech in isolated parts of Kentucky is that the people are speaking "Elizabethan" English. This popular belief is a little more difficult to refute, for Elizabethan English is technically modern English. Most of the words used in Elizabethan England are used today by English-speaking peoples. The shred of truth in the "Elizabethan" boast in Kentucky lies in the fact observed above—that one encounters more archaic words in a strongly traditional community than elsewhere. But rural Kentuckians today watch television, drive cars, go to the movies, eat potato chips, and talk about these things—hardly Elizabethan, let alone Anglo-Saxon.

Although popular beliefs about Kentucky speech still persist, sound scholarship on the subject began early. Dr. Eber C. Perrow, then head of the English department at the University of Louisville, was president of the Kentucky Folklore Society in 1916 and had been a prime mover in the society from its earlier years. His long serial article "Songs and Rhymes from the South" began in the *Journal of American Folklore* in 1912. His explanatory headnote included many sound observations about the language. Here he noted holp as the preterite for help, sont for sent, fotch for fetch, dove for dive, crope for creep, and many others. Some of the dialect items he listed referred to antique material culture, such as piggin (a small wooden vessel with one handle) and noggin (such a vessel with no handle).

Interestingly, Dr. Perrow had studied at Harvard University under the tutelage of the legendary George L. Kittredge, the scholar who edited the Kentucky mountain songs of schoolboy Josiah Combs. Kittredge had participated in the formation of the American Folklore Society at Harvard (in 1888 and thereafter). Perrow in Kentucky was carrying on the traditions of his famous mentor at Harvard.

Unfortunately for folklore study in Kentucky, Dr. Perrow fell into ill health in 1919 and, on medical advice, left the academic world to live in rural Georgia. In a communication printed by the *Kentucky Folklore Record* in 1957, he wrote:

From 1911–1919 I was head of the English department in the University of Louisville. While I was teaching there my wife and I, together with our three children, made our home out in the country in an old log cabin which we remodeled with our own hands. Here we came in close contact with the folk. . . . When, in 1919, ill health compelled me to leave academic work, I was glad to return to a life among the folk of the southern Appalachians where I since learned to make my living by farming rough mountain sides, and with a transit, relic of earlier studies in Civil Engineering, I have helped my neighbors keep their land lines moderately straight. In the meantime I have become a "snapper up" of a few "unconsidered trifles" of North Georgia folklore.

The idea of going to the country to live the simple life in a log house must have occurred to many a field-collecting folklorist, but Dr. Perrow appears to be the only one who has made such a permanent change of life. The fact that he had been a Kittredge pupil is more than mere coincidence. The fraternity of scholars who devote a considerable amount of their time and talent to serious consideration of folklore has always been a relatively small group. Many of them can trace their awareness and interest back to their professors in the same way one traces a family tree.

Perrow had acquired some of his training from Kittredge. Kittredge had been trained by his Harvard professor, Francis Child, the famed ballad scholar. Francis Child had studied in Germany, much under the influence of the brothers Grimm, universally known for their collections of folktales. The Grimm brothers are the end of the line, for their studies marked the real beginnings of academic work involving folk speech and folk literature. If one counts the generations, one might put Perrow down as a third-generation folklorist: the Grimms to Child; Child to Kittredge; Kittredge to Perrow. Also, the combined interest in both folk literature and the language of its conveyance holds true back to the beginning. Most people know the Grimm brothers in connection with folktales, but every college English major knows them also for Grimm's Law, a breakthrough in the formal study of linguistics—or philology, as it was known until recently.

Generations of folklorists have recognized the interdependence of the whole range of literature, all the way from the lowly folktale to the great masterpieces of poetry and drama. The Grimm brothers made contributions to the formal study of philology and mythology; Child's contemporaries would most likely have described him as an expert on British poetry, especially Spenser and Chaucer; Kittredge is best remembered for his Shakespeare classes; and Perrow's position as head of the English department at the University of Louisville is indicative of his stature.

The generations continue. Stith Thompson, another Kentucky native son, studied with Kittredge at Harvard and then went on to become recognized internationally as the principal American folktale scholar in the first half of the twentieth century. He ultimately retired as Distinguished Professor at Indiana University, but only after he had founded the first graduate program in folklore in the United States, a program which touched the lives of several other people associated with Kentucky folklore.

The earliest of the Thompson students from Kentucky was Gordon Wilson, Sr., a native of Calloway County, whose longest stay outside of Kentucky was his residence at Bloomington, Indiana, in pursuit of his doctorate. If one counts Thompson, like Perrow, as a third-generation folklorist in the Harvard genealogy, then Gordon Wilson was fourth-generation removed from the Grimms.

Gordon Wilson, like the members of the earlier generations, viewed language and literature as a continuum from the grassroots upward to the highest reaches of literature. During much of his mature career he was head of the English department at Western Kentucky University (designated as State College during much of his term). He is widely appreciated and remembered by many of his former students for his demanding course involving the history of the language. He is similarly appreciated and remembered by many residents of the Mammoth Cave region for his seemingly limitless curiosity about family names, place names, names of objects and actions, and all other kinds of words and phrases, for Gordon Wilson was one of those rarely fortunate individuals who manage to combine vocation and avocation.

Early in his career at Bowling Green, Wilson became interested in what he called "human ecology" in the Mammoth Cave region of Edmonson County. He was interested in what had happened to the region from the time it had been settled, and he was further interested in what would happen to the flora and fauna as a result of the old, worn-out farms being phased out as the national park developed. Since the region was near enough to his home to permit weekend and short vacation camping trips, he often spent the nights there in his sleeping bag. In the daytime he followed his twin hobbies, ornithology and philology, identifying a prothonotary warbler at one bend in the road, recording a place name such as Napper's Rollover at the next.

As the years went by, both kinds of collection grew. A bibliography compiled in 1968 showed that he had published 158 articles, notes, and pamphlets on ornithology. The same bibliography tallied about forty folklore titles. One of those entries, however, referred to *"Tidbits of Kentucky Folklore,* a series of articles published weekly since September, 1935, in approximately eighty newspapers." This adds up to about 1800 articles! If one multiplies by the number of outlets, the product is more than 140,000 separate exposures to the readers of Kentucky newspapers. Certainly his impact was a considerable one.

Yet "tidbits" suggests a kind of insubstantial froth, as indeed some popular treatments of folkways are. In his column, Gordon Wilson cheerfully shared the anecdotal and nostalgic bits for whatever entertainment value they might have, though he smuggled in bits of wisdom and philosophical speculation here and there. His greater contribution to scholarship is relatively unknown to the public who read his "Tidbits," for it is technical enough to be appreciated by the same kind of people who know about Grimm's Law.

The Gordon Wilson collection in the Western Kentucky University folklore archive consists of forty-eight seven-inch reels of tape recordings representing the speech of 240 of his Mammoth Cave region speakers. Abstracts from both tape recordings and informal questioning are located on 18,500 3 x 5 inch cards. Each card contains specific annotation, such as informant identification, variant spelling and pronunciation, and atlas, questionnaire, dictionary, or bibliographic references checked for the individual item. A conservative estimate of the number of separate transactions involved in the annotation of the card file would be well over 100,000.

As his collection grew, Gordon Wilson occasionally found time to abstract a particular cluster of related items to share with his colleagues. In the *Kentucky Folklore Record* appear such titles as "Mammoth Cave Words: Around the House," "Neighborhood Doings," "Some Good Regional Verbs," and "Some Useful Adjectives." In such articles he expounded on biggity, bigified, diked out, dumb-bull, flutter-mill, jewlarky, and moon-fixer. His comment on dumb-bull: "A noise-making contrivance made by attaching a fishing line to a nail in the bottom of a lard stand; a fishhook is attached to the other end of the string. When the hook is fastened to a window sash and a wad of *rozum* is rubbed on the taut string, enough noise to wake the dead is produced. Other names for this invention are *rozum the string, squeegie, horse fiddle,* or *tick-tack.*"

Late in his life, Gordon Wilson had the pleasure of sharing some of his great collection with like-minded scholars far from Kentucky. As scientific interest in regional speech developed, the ambitious project of preparing a dictionary which would show speech differentiation for all fifty states took shape, requiring that field workers make uniform sampling for all the areas represented. The *Dictionary of American Regional English,* usually shortened to *D.A.R.E.,* is still in preparation at the project headquarters in the University of Wisconsin under the direction of Dr. Frederic Cassidy.

"Word-wagon" was the name given to camper trucks especially outfitted for field collection in certain states where the dialect collectors would spend several weeks or months. The collectors were paid specialists, usually graduate students. With tape recorders, standardized questionnaires, and special procedures to insure sampling of speech in various geographical areas, balance of urban and rural speech, and representation of various age groups and levels of education, the field collectors gathered material to forward to headquarters periodically.

Sharon Huizinga, a tall, studious-looking graduate student from the University of Wisconsin, pulled her big word-wagon into Bowling Green in 1967. High on her list of priorities was the intent to visit with Gordon Wilson, whose research in folk speech was already known to Dr. Cassidy. Though nearly sixty years his junior, she found a kindred spirit in the spry, word-wise native of Calloway County. Partly as a result of his advice, she was off to a flying start in her Kentucky collection. Copies of her tape recordings of Kentuckians speaking are now a part of the general folklore archive at Western Kentucky University.

Dr. Cassidy himself came from Wisconsin to visit with the veteran Kentucky collector. His enthusiasm for the thousands of carefully documented cards was so great that he could not wait to delegate the task of copying selected items he wished to take with him to his Wisconsin headquarters. Accordingly, he rented the service of a fast-copying machine at a local business supply house, rolled up his sleeves, and with the aid of Gordon Wilson and a school secretary, copied hundreds of cards on the spot.

Later, for a special edition of essays to be presented on the occasion of Gordon Wilson's eightieth birthday, Dr. Cassidy wrote in part:

Work of this kind, done carefully and fully, is demanding—which perhaps explains why only a few achieve it. . . . There is no excuse hence-forward for anyone to make vague statements about "the way folks talk" in the Mammoth Cave area; if Gordon Wilson's materials are utilized, our statements can be quite particular and exact. This is the way we ought to be able to speak of local language matters, but far too seldom can. This is the difference between scholarly, scientific work and the superficial generalities to which we are too often reduced in areas not similarly studied.

But dialect study like this is not merely a matter of sound science. There has to be, in full measure, a human force behind it. Without enjoyment of one's fellow man, a real curiosity about the world and everything in it, without endless energy and patience, tasks of this kind are not accomplished. Anyone who knows Gordon Wilson or has made a field expedition with him will recognize the description. Suddenly the plain-seeming ground has geology underneath it, botany above it, ornithology flitting by (and quickly noted on a bird-watcher's card). Every hump and hollow turns out to have a name, sinks testify to hidden caves below, creeks thread their way in leaf-vein patterns. And connected with each is an anecdote, a trenchant thought, a phrase of poetry or literature aptly recalled. Everything is more alive than it was before, "far more deeply interfused" by mind and heart.

Though no other small area in Kentucky has been studied in depth as intensely and as long as the Mammoth Cave region, other parts of the state are represented in a variety of ways by serious observers of language habits. Place names, for example, are of interest both for the names themselves and for the legends, beliefs, or practices associated with them. Monkey's Eyebrow turns up regularly in jocular newspaper allusions. Lickskillet (Logan County) seems peculiar enough to be unique, but it is shared as a place name with Indiana. Turnhole Bend (Green River) is puzzling until one discovers that "turnhole" is just a good descriptive folk name for "whirlpool." Leonard Roberts has capitalized on colorful names for creeks and hollows in eastern Kentucky in his book titles: Cutshin, Greasy, Hell-fer-Sartin. John Fetterman was similarly attracted to Stinking Creek. In the Mammoth Cave area alone are such colorful and sometimes puzzling names as Blowing Spring, Ugly Creek, Tom Johns Crossing, Crump's Goblin, Lick Log, and Stillhouse Hollow.

The persistence of specialized vocabulary indicates the persistence of the activity associated with it. By conducting an inquiry into the vocabulary of marbles in nineteen eastern Kentucky counties, Edward M. White indirectly verified that the traditional game is alive and well in that part of the state. Reporting his findings in the 1963 volume of the *Kentucky Folklore Record,* he reminded readers of such terms as blue-goose, chippie, dough-roller, fats, granny-hole, haydoodle, knucks, lag, nudges, pee-wee, stick-in, taw, and tribs. He collected 186 traditional terms used in playing marbles, and he was able to show highly localized usage, with some terms differing in adjacent counties. Hikes, for example, is used in Letcher, Johnson, Lewis, Carter, Greenup, and Boyd counties, but knucks has identical use in the vocabularies found in Perry, Pike, and Greenup counties. Apparently, both terms were collected in Greenup. Although the regular name for the game, marbles, occurred in most of the counties, the alternate term marvels was reported for eight of the counties surveyed. Brief studies of this kind help illustrate the mechanics of dialect differentiation in a living language.

The persistence of an activity, of course, implies the presence of specialized vocabulary enabling participants and interested bystanders to communicate or interact. Involving social as well as simply regional variation are such persistent activities in the commonwealth as illegal whiskey-making and horse racing. It was inevitable that Dr. David W. Maurer, University of Louisville English professor and widely known authority on the language of the underworld, would take scholarly note of the argot of moonshining, the racetrack, and other activities which have generated an interesting specialized vocabulary in his region. Although his studies have ranged geographically far beyond Kentucky, his contributions on subjects that have a special local significance have enriched the literature of Kentucky folk speech.

Regional words fall into patterns in traditional song and story, but Kentucky superstitions, curses, blessings, polite greeting and leave-taking, proverbial comparisons, proverbs, and riddles also assume special localized characteristics. Not everyone creates an ear-catching phrase, but many who do are imitated; thus a particular usage develops in a particular region.

A southern leave-taking commonly heard in Kentucky is "Y-all come back. Hear?" Out of this comes the joke about a stranger to the custom confused because he thought he heard "Y-all come back here!" He promptly returned. Josiah Combs contributed a humorous exchange on greeting and leave-taking to *Kentucky Folklore Record* (1957). Though intentionally overdrawn, it is still a valid comment on a regional feeling that it is impolite to greet a friend or acquaintance briefly. A man sits on his porch; another passes:

"Howdy, Samp?"
"Howdy, Sam?"
"Won't ye g'down awhile?"
"Cain't, I reckon; got to be gittin' on down the road."
"Better 'light an' show ye saddle?"
"Hain't got time, I guess."
"Ye mought as well a-stopped."
" 'D like to, but 'pears like I cain't; won't ye g'long down?"
"Couldn't, I reckon."
(Looking upward) "B'lieve we're goin' t'have a little rain." (This as he rides away.)
"The elemints does look threatenin'."
"Fix to bring the old woman down and stay a spell with us."
"Been a-layin' off to come, a good spell. You come up and stay awhile with us."
"I will, you come."
"All right, you come."

Why do so many folks say "Dead as four o'clock"? Is it four o'clock in the morning, or four o'clock in the evening, or not a time of day at all? Does the saying refer to the flower called four o'clock? If so, why dead? One wonders who invented the simile and why others use it.

Similarly, many Kentuckians speak of a widow who is beginning to be interested in courtship in an earthy way, using familiar barnyard imagery: "Her comb's getting red." The saying has been used long enough to extend its application to young people beginning to be interested in the opposite sex. These and many other sayings remain in oral tradition even though writers occasionally dip into the reservoir and use them for their regional flavor.

Beliefs are also a part of the oral tradition. Most of the beliefs (or superstitions) expressed in Kentucky are ancient and widespread—even world-wide. Those that are purely regional are often associated with particular places or events. Only one large sampling of Kentucky superstitions has appeared in print. This is *Kentucky Superstitions* by Daniel L. and Lucy Thomas in 1920. Daniel Thomas, incidentally, is credited with being the founder of the Kentucky Folklore Society. Like Josiah Combs, Thomas had international experience. A native of Lebanon, Kentucky, he received his Ph.D. in English at Princeton University, studied at Oxford University in England, the Sorbonne in France, and the University of Munich in Germany. He was head of the English department at Centre College at the time of his death in 1920, and *Kentucky Superstitions* was completed and seen into print (Princeton University Press) by his sister. The collection contains 3,954 numbered superstitions found in the state. Thus Thomas No. 2510: If a fire sighs, there will be a very cold spell of weather; Thomas No. 1935: To dream of unbroken eggs is a sign of trouble to come; and Thomas No. 3624: If you turn your left shoe bottom side up against the table leg, it will stop a shivering owl.

During the generations of rural isolation, riddling was a cherished pastime for adults and children alike. A good stock of riddles, like a good stock of recitations and songs, was an envied possession of the fireside wit. Only in recent times has riddling been thought of as primarily children's activity. A 1973 publication of the Kentucky Folklore Society reveals, however, that at least some Kentucky adults still have a good repertoire. *Riddles from the Cumberland Valley* by Charles S. Guthrie is a special publication, Kentucky Folklore Series No. 5. This collection of 124 riddles from eleven informants in Cumberland County contains a perceptive introduction by William Hugh Jansen, who remarks:

Any contest will draw spectators, and as does any other kind of contest, this one affords the opportunity to identify with either contestant. The direction of the identification depends, naturally, on whether the identifier knows the answer before it is given in the present procedure. The joy and excitement of competition is frequently latent in the very wording of the riddle. . . .

One other reason for the longevity of the riddle lies in the probable frequency of its performance. It takes talent and a kind of confidence to tell a story or sing a song to a critical, knowing audience. Many folk communities do not include a single member who is considered a singer or a narrator, but generally I think it is felt that anyone can perform a riddle. . . . Then riddles survive because theirs is, in a way, a more democratic genre than most.

Of the riddles Jansen designates as having a folk aesthetic quality, Guthrie's No. 46 is a good example:

As I went through a field of wheat,
I picked up something good to eat.
'Twas neither fish, flesh, fowl, or bone.
I kept it until it ran alone.
(Partridge's or quail's egg)

More recently James Still has produced an attractively illustrated small volume entitled *Way Down Yonder on Troublesome Creek: Appalachian Riddles & Rusties.* Still, long noted for his carefully crafted short stories set in rural eastern Kentucky, has been quite selective, choosing mainly the rhymed riddles, the kind Jansen thinks of as having aesthetic quality.

Examination of a large collection of these smaller expressions which range from the word or phrase to a rhymed riddle or proverb suggests strongly that there is, indeed, a folk aesthetic. It is not the man of letters only who appreciates metaphor and colorful simile; the unlettered seize upon them instinctively. In fact, more often than the man of letters likes to admit, everyday work in barn and field rather than in study and library is the source of spontaneous, natural imagery.

4

THE YARNSPINNER
IN KENTUCKY

LEONARD ROBERTS, a tireless collector of old-fashioned folktales in eastern Kentucky, contributed "Polly, Nancy, and Muncimeg" to the 1955 volume of *Kentucky Folklore Record*, and thereby illustrated the problem of identifying Kentucky tales. In his note on the tale, Roberts indicated that he had collected it from Tom Couch, age ninety-two, in Harlan County. After recording the Tom Couch version (in writing because there was no electricity for a tape recorder), Roberts tape-recorded a version from Tom's son Jim, age fifty-two.

The tale is about three girls who receive an inheritance. Two of the girls receive the valuable property, while the other (the youngest-best) receives only an old pocket penknife and a gold ring. The apparently worthless objects have magical properties, however, so that Muncimeg gets out of numerous scrapes by invoking them. She succeeds finally in outwitting the giant and returns to the king's house, where "She got the king's youngest son for a husband, and they all went back home and lived happy."

This brief sketch reflects many of the elements of Old-World folktales: adventures or quests, success of the youngest-best, magical objects or incantations, giants or other fearsome creatures, and the cliché happy ending. Roberts notes that the story "is one of those close and probably older versions of 'Jack and the Beanstalk.' " He also remarks on parallel versions collected by Richard Chase and others. The problem: How *Kentucky* is this version of an ancient European tale? One way to answer is to ask another question: How *Kentucky* are these people descended from old European families?

The settlers of Kentucky brought their language, songs, and stories with them, and just as the people have gradually become Kentuckians instead of displaced natives of England, Scotland, Ireland, and other European and African places, so the tales that survive through the generations adapt to their new cultural setting.

"Polly, Nancy, and Muncimeg," as reported by Leonard Roberts, contains language and allusions never found in Europe. The episode in which the heroine escapes from a sack after being tied up by the giant illuminates:

He went out to get him a frail to frail her with. She said "Law me, my momy's old pocket penknife and gold ring," and down come the sack and out she come. She caught his old dog and cat and put 'em in the sack and rounded up all his knives and forks, teacups and saucers. Put 'em all in the sack and hung it back up to the joist. She got out beside the house and listened for him.

The folktale has adapted to its Kentucky environment. This is generally true of other tales in the Roberts collection. His *South from Hell-fer-Sartin, Up Cutshin and Down Greasy,* and *Old Greasybeard* reflect his skill and energy as a collector of tales that seem oddly out of place in mid-twentieth century. His careful annotations reveal that these old-fashioned tales, like the old Scottish ballads, are no longer widely known and narrated. They tend to cluster, rather, in remote communities and in the story-telling traditions of particular families, as illustrated by the similar narrations of Tom Couch and his son Jim.

Leonard Roberts received some of his folklore indoctrination at Indiana University, so he, like Gordon Wilson, might be identified as four generations removed from the Grimm ancestry of folktale scholarship. Another Stith Thompson student collected Kentucky folktales before Leonard Roberts began, but published them at a much later date. Marie Campbell taught at the mountain settlement school on Caney Creek in Knott County in 1926. The following year she moved to Gander (now Carcasonne) in Letcher County. The isolation of this community in the 1920s is indicated in her description—a day-long journey in a jolt-wagon "across mountains and creeks with folk names: Troublesome, Betty's Troublesome, Defeated. . . ."

Up to 1934, the last year she taught at Gander, she closely observed the life of the community and collected songs, tales, and customs. One of her early publications was the description of an old folk drama resurrected out of the memories of the people in the community and performed as a special favor for her. She also published ballads in *Southern Folklore Quarterly*, but her folktale manuscripts lay dormant until 1953, when she began studies for her doctorate at Indiana University. Encouraged by Stith Thompson, she transcribed and annotated seventy-eight tales for her dissertation, published in 1958 by Indiana University Press as *Tales of the Cloud Walking Country*.

The volume is a compilation of the folktale stock of Aunt Lisbeth Fields, Big Nelt, Uncle Tom Dixon, Doc Rourk, Uncle Blessing, and Sam Caudill. Her annotations refer eighteen times to tales in Leonard Roberts's *South from Hell-fer-Sartin*, a useful reference, for, as she points out in her introduction, his tales "were collected in counties of the eastern Kentucky region, similar to the area from which my collection comes." The limited number of informants supports the observation that not every member of a folk community is a talented storyteller or singer. While many people may be familiar with the material, relatively few (like the few novelists or poets in the world of written literature) can give a good rendition. This is an explanation of the disappointment a student collector sometimes experiences when he tries to collect folktales. If he assumes that just anyone can tell a tale, he may get a poor, truncated fragment—a *report of* a folktale rather than the fully developed, well-told item. But if the collector understands that most informants are not artists and he succeeds in tracing the report of a tale back to its source, he may find himself in the presence of a Tom Couch or an Aunt Lisbeth Fields.

Leonard Roberts and Marie Campbell have contributed much to an understanding of oral literature in Kentucky, but it would be an error to expect the quaint Old-World *Märchen* to persist indefinitely in the space age. Even at the time of their collection these tales were localized anachronisms. *Märchen* are rarely collected in western Kentucky. The international tale-types that persist relate to contemporary beliefs, attitudes, or preoccupations.

Even more persistent than identifiable tale-types (such as "Snow White" or "Cinderella") are what folktale scholars call *motifs,* narrative elements that are not whole tales but which seem to have an independent life of their own, turning up solo sometimes as brief anecdotes or expressions of belief, but more commonly combining with other motifs, sometimes in surprisingly new settings. The motifs of magic objects, magic words, wicked stepmothers, and jealous older siblings are familiar enough to be recognizable everywhere.

A good example of an old motif brought up to date is the story of a duck hunter near Horse Cave. He was walking along the edge of a deep gully with a stream flowing along its bottom. The hunter spied a flock of ducks in a pool, but he was so high above them that he couldn't approach near enough for a shot without causing them to take flight. He went back upstream to a large patch of pumpkins he had noticed earlier. He threw a few small pumpkins into the stream and let them float down to get the ducks used to the idea. Then he hollowed out a large one like a Jack-o'-Lantern, put it over his head, and waded in. Thus disguised, he waded through the flock of ducks like a floating pumpkin, calmly catching them by their legs until he had as many as he could hold. He had underestimated their lifting power, however, so that when they finally became alarmed and took flight, they carried him up with them. Cool-headed, he waited until the ducks had carried him to the upper rim so that he wouldn't have to climb out, then wrung a few necks to let himself down easy, and went home with his game.

The motif of being carried through the air by wildfowl is an old one with many variations. It is in the tradition of tall tales about hunting that are very much a part of the American frontier. This motif appeared among the exploits of Baron Münchausen, suggesting old European origins. It may have been introduced into the American scene by a literary translation, and it has been used by William Gilmore Simms. Nevertheless, it has a lively oral tradition, the Horse Cave version being somewhat different from any other.

In Logan County a rural couple had a toddler named Ruthie who had not been weaned from her bottle. She would come to her mother to have the bottle filled, then wander around drinking through the nursing nipple. Her parents gradually began to notice that Ruthie was going directly to the woodshed when she had her bottle filled. Following her one day, they were horrified to discover the little girl feeding her milk to an enormous rattlesnake that had crawled out of the woodpile. The child was petting the snake and crooning to it as it fed. The parents carefully sneaked up to avoid alarming the snake, killed it, and snatched their daughter away. After that incident, Ruthie was strangely withdrawn, then finally fell into a critical illness. She recovered but was never right in the head afterward.

Perhaps because Kentucky has a considerable reptile population, tales about snakes—both real and mythical—turn up at every hand. Copperheads and rattlesnakes are likely to intrude in any extended conversation relating to outdoor activities. Though the folk names for joint, hoop, and coachwhip snakes apply to real reptiles, the fearsome biological characteristics attributed to them exist only in folk fancy.

The Logan County snake tale is very old, probably originating in India, where the child's reptile friend would be a cobra instead of a rattlesnake. Kentucky versions are generally told as true (or "belief") tales.

A Hart County narration concerns the adventure of a young man on his first deer hunting excursion. His father, who was hunting with him, warned him that if he shot a deer and didn't claim it immediately, some bully might put a tag on it and claim it as his kill. The boy and his father separated, and shortly thereafter the boy shot a deer. He had to go to his father for a tag. When they returned to the scene, a carload of ugly-acting city hunters had claimed the deer. Fortunately, a game warden came by, and it fell his lot to judge the dispute. The city hunters loudly argued that they had killed the deer and had not left the scene. The boy then asked them to produce the deer's tongue. When they looked and found none, the boy dramatically produced the deer's tongue from his pocket, proof that he had been there first.

This is another hunting tale told as a true happening, which it *could* be. The motif of the missing tongue, however, comes from an old European folktale, "The Dragonslayer," in which the seven tongues of a slain seven-headed dragon are produced just as dramatically to prove which is the real hero and which is the impostor. As long as hunting continues to be a popular pastime in Kentucky there will be many opportunities to combine old motifs with local yarns, some of which will be told as sober truth, while others will be clearly in the big lie tradition.

An example of the latter category is the tale of the beagle so smart that he herded a covey of quail into a groundhog hole, sat on the hole until his owner came, then released the birds one at a time so that the hunter could shoot them on the wing as if he were trapshooting.

Brief folktales of this kind received relatively little attention until a spurt of activity in the 1950s marked a kind of renaissance of the Kentucky Folklore Society. Much of this activity can be attributed to interest generated by Leonard Roberts and Marie Campbell, but other folklorists trained by Stith Thompson also arrived on the scene. Herbert Halpert initiated wide-scale collecting at Murray State University, while William Hugh Jansen was similarly engaged at the University of Kentucky.

Halpert and Jansen gave emphasis to a new phase in the study of Kentucky folklore. Whereas earlier scholars had relied on their own energies and spare time to collect and annotate folkloristic materials, Halpert and Jansen were able to extend their reach enormously by enlisting the aid of interested students. Their access to students was facilitated by introduction of folklore courses at their respective schools.

With the arrival of Halpert and Jansen (and later D. K. Wilgus at Western Kentucky University) came the recognition of the need for systematic archiving of texts of all kinds. A single rendition of a folktale is fine as a curiosity or as grist for the journalistic mill, but many texts are needed for comparative study so that sound generalizations can be made about the material. Willing helpers with access to willing informants in their homes and communities, then, make the task easier.

Halpert at Murray and Jansen at Lexington contributed a steady flow of notes, texts, theories, and conclusions, both to the *Kentucky Folklore Record* and to other regional and national journals. They also helped correct an imbalance that had warped the image of Kentuckians from the beginning—overemphasis on mountain material. Kentucky mountain folklore was still being collected and studied by such people as Marie Campbell, Leonard Roberts, and Cratis Williams (at Appalachian State College). But Halpert's thrust reached all the way to the Mississippi to the west, and Jansen's know-how shed new light on Bluegrass folklore.

Although the emphasis given here to the Grimm-Child-Kittredge-Thompson line of influence is justified in light of the product at the end of the line, it would be inappropriate to suggest that this was the only line of transmission. For one thing, Kittredge and Child at Harvard had many students, disciples who fanned out in all directions, so that their combined influence is difficult to trace. While Stith Thompson was planting the folk studies seed at Indiana University, for example, his classmate Archer Taylor was doing the same at Berkeley. Another example is Duncan Emrich, the last student Kittredge supervised for a Ph.D. degree, who pioneered in many kinds of collection, archiving, and publication of American folklore. His *Folklore on the American Land* (1972) makes liberal use of collected Kentucky materials, thereby aiding in placing Kentucky folklore in proper perspective in the national scene. Though neither Taylor nor Emrich resided in Kentucky, both of them contributed to the growing body of literature that explains the oral traditions of the state.

At the same time Halpert and Jansen were bringing new authority to folk studies in Kentucky, two other men displayed remarkably versatile talents as they fed a steady stream of language notes and bibliographical items into the rejuvenated society publication.

One of these is Hensley C. Woodbridge, one-time librarian at Murray State University and editor of *Kentucky Folklore Record* from 1962 to 1964. Woodbridge pooled his talents with those of D. K. Wilgus in the 1950s to produce an annual bibliography of Kentucky folklore, and he continues to serve on the board of directors of the Kentucky Folklore Society.

The other is Lawrence S. Thompson, formerly librarian and more recently professor in the Department of Classics at the University of Kentucky. Thompson, too, is a versatile and tireless annotator. His *Kentucky Tradition* (1956) brings attention to several valid aspects of Kentucky traditional life which have been neglected by other folklorists. Titles of five of his twenty-one chapters illustrate how much more widely his interest ranged: "Politics as a Major Sport," "Laws, Lawyers, and the Legislature," "His Equine Majesty," "The Sporting Tradition," and "Calvinists, Catholics, and Campbellites." *Kentucky Tradition,* crammed with anecdotes and fully documented for sources, many of which are virtually unknown to the general reader, is a valuable and different sourcebook.

In *Kentucky Tradition* Thompson related the anecdote of a Kentucky Negro minister baptizing by immersion. The minister was a small man, and one of his candidates was too large for him to hold. The unsupported candidate floundered in the river until he could pull himself up, then shouted at the minister, "Look heah, you'd better quit this 'ere foolishness; de fust ting you know you'll drown some gen'lmun's valuable thousan' dollah niggah."

These Negroes, Thompson remarks, are "about as real as Old Black Joe." Of course, the reality of characters in folktales, black or white, is no criterion for either the reality or the popularity of oral fiction, but Kentucky folktales about black people bring up some interesting problems. Consider this widely circulated tale about a hunting episode:

A group of Bowling Green hunters got their guns, lanterns, ropes, and shovels for a nocturnal possum hunt. Of course they brought along a colored man to carry their gear. They had a good hunt. By midnight they had traveled several miles and had four possums. The hunters were tired and decided to build a fire and rest, so they asked the colored man to gather wood, build a fire, and skin a possum to eat. Having done all the work, he was so tired that he fell sound asleep by the fire.

When the possum was done, the hunters ate it up, then, for a joke, greased the colored man's hands and mouth and laid the pile of bones beside him. When he awoke, he smelled his hands, looked at the bones, and said, "Well, I might of eat that possum, but if I did, it done me the least good of any possum I ever ate in my life."

"Colored man" tales are traditional in the tale-telling repertoire of both white and black raconteurs, as amply illustrated in Richard Dorson's *American Negro Folktales*. In recent years of militant civil rights most of these tales have fallen into disrepute for either oral or written rendition. Many are objectionable because of gross racial caricature. Yet their existence is a fact of folklore to be reckoned with in any thoughtful assessment of the role of the folktale in establishing or maintaining social stereotypes. With the decline of acceptance of such tales, the old-fashioned orator, a stock figure in Kentucky politics, must drastically revise his inventory of anecdotes.

Since there is no militant resistance to making jokes about poor whites, the gross caricature of the moonshiner or feuding mountaineer is still acceptable. It is interesting to observe that some of these tales would be objectionable if they were to contain an allusion to color, but they are acceptable if the butt of the joke is assumed to be white. In fact, some tales widely enough collected to reveal variant texts may have an ignorant or superstitious white as the butt of the joke in one text, a Negro in another. Here are examples provided to *Kentucky Folklore Record* by Josiah Combs:

A traveler stopped to chat with a mountaineer who lived on top of a mountain, miles distant from the nearest habitation or country store.

Traveler: Isn't it rather difficult to obtain the necessities of life up here so far away from everything?

Mountaineer: Yeah, hit shorely is, and even when you git 'em they ain't fitten to drink.

An industrial school was being founded at Hindman, in Knott County. The ladies delegated to start the school were from the lowlands. The trip from the nearest railway station, at Jackson, required two days in order to reach Hindman, and the ladies were traveling in a rough jolt-wagon, over rough, dirt roads. They stopped at a mountaineer's home the first night. The beds were in one room. The mountaineer's wife watched, with great curiosity, the ladies undress and put on their sleeping garments before retiring.

"Do ye all do this every night before ye go to bed?" she asked them. On being told that they did, she paused for several seconds, then: "Ye all must be a lot of trouble to yeselves."

Although the tales are not complimentary to their subjects, there is no suggestion of malice in their rendition. The fact is that all brief anecdotes of this type must have a target for the humor, be it the Irish immigrant, the farmer's daughter, the preacher, the Polish bridegroom, or the psychiatrist. In Kentucky the hapless hillman, unprotected by organized resistance, seems the most likely candidate to go on feudin', fightin', and fussin'.

An aspect of Kentucky which has not been fully assessed is the close tie between anecdotal lore and political life. There is a general awareness of traditional socializing in Kentucky around the courthouse square.

Governors, legislators, lawyers, and judges are identified as especially good raconteurs. Kentucky historian Thomas D. Clark, whose skillful and perceptive use of folklore should make any folklorist envious, wrote, "No social historian will ever be able to determine how many Kentucky political battles have been fought and refought at the dinner table. . . . Scores of students of folk literature have invaded the Kentucky mountains to search eagerly for snatches of English ballads, but they have overlooked that more important oasis of folk culture known as 'Kentucky dinner talk' " (*The Kentucky*).

Some Kentucky writers have been alert to this kind of material. Irvin S. Cobb's Judge Priest was a literary creation precisely suited to exploitation of a particular image of Kentucky. William H. Townsend, Kentucky orator, lawyer, and historian, striking an autobiographical pose, delivered a broad slice of Kentucky social history and folklore in his *Hundred Proof: Salt River Sketches and Memoirs of the Bluegrass*. It is significant that historians cherish Townsend's tape-recorded delivery of some of this material, a suggestion that, in this instance at least, the distinction between oral and written literature is more a matter of medium than of content.

The fully adequate study is yet to be made on Kentucky dinner talk and courthouse talk. When it is made, it may prove more valuable to understanding Kentucky folklore than any pursuit of the vanishing *Märchen*.

5

FOLK HISTORY
AND LEGENDS

THE GREAT OCEAN of world story rolled on for centuries, and the lore of millennia was preserved in human memory before man invented writing systems. A recognition of language as symbol is as essential to the folklorist as to the poet. Accounts of experiences involving humor, tragedy, loyalties, group solidarity—things that matter to individuals and small groups—may not find a place in historical documents or belletristic literature, but persistence in oral tradition is testimonial enough of their continuing force. In an era of almost universal literacy this rather obvious truth may be overlooked. A classroom anecdote illustrates the crippling effect of forgetting that the miracle of writing came after the greater miracle of language.

A literature professor was expounding on the poetry of the sacred chants of a North American Indian tribe. A puzzled student raised her hand.

"How could they have poetry if they had no writing?" The student could not think about poetry without visualizing a printed page or words arranged in lines with an uneven right-hand margin. The professor made some little marks on the blackboard.

"What are these little marks?" he asked.

"Rain," was the prompt response.

"They don't look like rain to me," he said, squinting critically at the blackboard. "They look more like . . . smears of chalk dust on a black surface."

"But it *says* rain," the student insisted.

"I'm listening," the professor said, cupping his ear toward the blackboard. "I can't hear it say anything."

"Well, it *represents*," the student muttered, exasperated. "It's all the same."

"If it only represents, then it must be a substitute," the professor said patiently. "I'm sorry to act so obtuse, but we should recognize that the spoken word came first, and little marks on paper are sometimes a pretty poor substitute for the voice." He went on through the familiar routine, showing that even the spoken word was not *rain*, but rather, a mere noise serving as a local symbol for the natural fact. Then he worked his way back to the observation that the spoken word served for all literature and history before the recent invention of writing, and that with all its magic of inflection and mimicry, it is far superior to writing for many purposes, especially for poetry.

This little classroom exercise is appropriate for review when one compares oral history with written history, and especially when one thinks about folk history. The folk are not preoccupied with the fine, hair-splitting distinctions that are so much a part of academic life. The academic historian is necessarily involved with voluminous papers, books, documents, and other kinds of recorded facts. He could not do his work without them. In his preoccupation with the necessary paraphernalia of his profession, he may, like the student confusing the shadow of poetry on a printed page for the real thing, insist that history must be a written record.

Yet things happen. People live, love, struggle, vanquish, or are vanquished, and they tell about it. They tell about their own experience and the experience of others, and sometimes the telling is interrupted by

45

"That's not the way I heard it!" The oral historian finds almost limitless opportunities for scholarly analysis in the vast body of unwritten materials relating to Kentucky politics. These are not always accounts of important events and people. They do not reach the pages of printed books or other written documents, but they can add a whole new dimension to the understanding of the spirit of a time and a place. Hugh M. Thomason, a professor of government at Western Kentucky University, has amassed such a body of this abundant material that mere classification has become a problem.

"Yes, I bought votes at several different elections," old Carl Smith said to the inquiring student. "In those days it was two dollars a vote, but I've bought many a vote for a dollar apiece when there was a good turnout and I didn't have but so much money to give out."

"Where did you get the money?"

"Why, whoever was running for office. I remember the time Tom Butterfield was running for legislature. He come to my house, says, 'Carl, here's two hundred dollars. I wish you would go over to Crossroads tomorrow and see if anybody there needs help.' So I went. Rode my horse over to the church first thing in the morning and stayed all day."

"Did they vote in the church?"

"Oh, no. They voted at the postoffice them days. But the church was just catty-corner across from there. You wouldn't want to go hanging around the polling place, you know."

"How did people know you were there? And how did they know what you wanted?"

"Well, word gets around. Besides, either me or somebody else was always there at every election, so people would know. Now, anybody that votes knows which side I'm on, so he'd know what I was paying for, and he wouldn't come and ask if he hadn't voted right."

"How would you know?"

46

"Just know. These are honest people. They wouldn't cheat. If a neighbor comes and says, 'I voted right today, and I sure could use a dollar or two,' why, then I'd know I owed it. You see, I never did go out and grab a voter and say, 'I'll pay you two dollars to vote right.' That would be real bad. But if a good neighbor comes by and says, 'I could use a dollar or two,' I'm glad to help him. Now, the time Butterfield ran there was such a big turnout, I ran out of money before the polls closed, and I was sorry for it. Here come old Uncle Lou Harrison—fine old man, never had much, and he says, 'I sure could use a couple of dollars,' and I says, 'I'm sorry, Uncle Lou, I've run out of money,' and he says, 'I would be just as happy for only a dollar, or even fifty cents,' and I didn't have it. Made me feel so cheap I got on my horse and rode on home."

This narrative, slightly modified for locale and personalities, illustrates a facet of Kentucky political life at the grassroots level. As Kentucky history it is so minute and particular that it can claim little attention from the historian or political scientist—a check mark, perhaps, to indicate one more verification of vote-buying in Kentucky. But it means more than vote-buying, for it reveals certain attitudes and values that can be a key to understanding activities other than voting.

The narrative shows that buying votes seemed more normal than abnormal to Carl Smith. Judging by his reported success, it also seemed normal to the voters. Smith alludes to the honesty of the people he paid. He could trust them to do the right thing. They, in turn, trusted him. The fact that candidates would seek him out regularly to dispense money shows that they trusted him to pay it out rather than pocket it. The implication is that Smith enjoyed a somewhat higher status in the voting district than most other citizens.

It is clear that he did not go about the polling place soliciting and that he did not offer bribes. He could, however, generously respond to people who asked for a favor. But it is also clear that both Smith and the voters understood their activity to be legalistic evasion.

As the analysis develops, some idea of a double standard of honesty begins to emerge. People scrupulous to the penny in everyday transactions feel no shame about shady transactions in politics. The closing lines of James H. Mulligan's verse in *All That's Kentucky* come to mind:

> *Mountains tower proudest,*
> *Thunder peals the loudest,*
> *The landscape is the grandest,*
> *And politics the damndest*
> *In Kentucky.*

Oral history as expressed by ordinary folk increasingly attracts the attention of folklorists, not for the reliability of events reported therein, but for improving and extending insights about the content and function of all oral traditions. The very qualities that make the conventional historian wary of oral history—embellishment and inaccuracy—are the ones that generate interest in other quarters. How embellished? Why inaccurate?

Many influences go to work on the remembered event, and the farther it travels by oral transmission, the more it may be affected by the aesthetics and biases of its successive narrators. In addition to the inevitable changes wrought by misunderstanding and faulty memory, oral history may be reshaped by an aesthetic urge to make the telling sound "right" according to some standard of oratory and imagery. The ego may also intrude as the narrator seeks to make either the event or his role in it more important than the facts warrant, or the reverse of this, to diminish his role in an action he cannot be proud of.

The most interesting alteration to the folklorist, and the one he is best equipped to verify, is the incorporation of an identifiable narrative motif into an otherwise straightforward account. It is this kind of alteration that tested the judgment of William Lynwood Montell in the preparation of *The Saga of Coe Ridge: A Study in Oral History* (University of Tennessee Press, 1970).

Montell is yet another Kentucky native son who went to Indiana University for graduate work in folklore. Because he was already familiar with the area of Cumberland County which is the subject of the *Saga*, he chose to study the Coe Ridge community for his doctoral dissertation. The book, a significant, pioneering work, is a publication of the dissertation.

The subject of Montell's study is a tiny colony on the Kentucky-Tennessee border near the Cumberland River. Since the Civil War it has been known as Coetown or Zeketown. Its Negro population was originally made up of freed slaves of an owner named Coe. Because the ridge was so inaccessible it gradually became a refuge for moonshiners and other lawbreakers. Mixture of the races on the ridge added to the indignation of white people in surrounding communities, who desired elimination of what some of them considered to be a social blight in the area. Not until good roads finally penetrated the wilderness in the 1930s did the ridge cease to give refuge to fugitives.

Coe Ridge had provided scanty records for conventional historical treatment, and some of those had been destroyed by a courthouse fire. The tape recorder, then, became Montell's principal research tool. He tracked down descendants of both the black and the white Coes; he interviewed townspeople in the region; he interviewed law enforcement officials. His is a study in oral history; it is also a study in Kentucky folklore.

By collating different accounts of the same events, Montell was able to arrive at reasonably reliable accounts of what actually occurred in many instances. By being alert to traveling anecdotes, he was able to identify narrative intrusions in others. An example of embellishment deriving from a folk belief appears in the account of Simp Smith being murdered by Big Les: "Although Big Les finally admitted killing Simp Smith, the inhabitants of Zeketown and their white neighbors knew. . . . Blood oozed from the corpse when Big Les walked up and looked at it." In a footnote Montell observes that the telltale blood motif is recorded as a widespread folk belief.

Another set of intrusions concerned the supernatural strength of Bill Zeke Coe. Various informants attributed to him the following feats: carrying a log other men could not lift in unison, holding up a wagon so other men could repair its wheel, holding up two trees at the same time, and carrying a wagon on his shoulders. Montell identifies some of these strong-man motifs as items reported elsewhere about other people.

A "panther on the roof" narration came from one Coe Ridge informant. The story relates how women stayed up all night throwing bones and scraps of food out through the logs of their house to placate a hungry panther. Montell notes that the "panther on the roof" tale is discussed by J. Frank Dobie in *Tales of Old-Time Texas* and by Mody Boatright in *The Family Saga and Other Phases of American Folklore.* Boatright, he observes, thought the Texas tales had derived from Tennessee at an early date.

This observation indicates that the "panther on the roof" episode, though a part of the oral history of the Coe family, is not factual. It is functional, however, for the folk act upon what they believe to be true, or even upon what they choose to believe, rather than upon what they can verify. The folklore of a community, like the literature of a nation, provides models for behavior. In the long, bloody feud between the Zeketown people and certain white factions off the ridge, shooting, ambush, seige, stabbing, and even throat-cutting occur with depressing regularity, but intermingled are daring, endurance, and even a streak of chivalry here and there:

And [Taylor] just rode right on by them—never spoke or let on like the boys wudn't there. Just went right on by them.

And one of these fellows said after he passed, said, "I'm going to shoot him right in the cross of the galluses."

And this fellow's brother said there, "If you do, I'll shoot you. A man that's got nerve enough to do that, they ain't nobody going to shoot him in the back where I am."

What should be called legend and what should be called oral history appears to depend on how the material is to be treated. Montell himself refers to many of his narratives as legends. His treatment of them, however, is historical; that is, he uses careful collection, collation, and analysis of legendary material for the purpose of gaining historical insights. Any one of the separate narratives about Coe Ridge on the tape recordings deposited in the Western Kentucky University Folklore Archive would be called a folk legend, a narrative about a person, place, or event purported to be true. Many tales of the supernatural fall into this category. The following tale related from family tradition by a Johnson County resident is a good example.

You've heard of haunted houses, and maybe you don't believe in 'em. Now this one is a *real* haunted house tale. My brother-in-law's sister and her sister lived over here on Pond Creek at a little place called Blackberry, up Blackberry Creek, and they was a big farm up there and a big house on it, but no one would live in it. It was haunted and nobody wouldn't live in it. So this brother-in-law's brother-in-law, his name was Joe, got out of a job, and my brother-in-law went to him and told him of this place.

"Now," he said, "if you want to live up there, it's free. It won't cost you a penny if you'll stay in it." But he said, "No one has ever stayed in that house."

"What's the matter with it?" Joe said.

Said, "It's haunted."

"I don't believe in it," he said, "I don't believe in haints, so I'll take it."

51

Well, they moved in and Joe put out his crops. It was along in July before, well, they'd heard some noises, but they didn't pay any attention to 'em and ignored 'em. So long about the time crops were maturing, why, one night they went to bed, and they heard chains begin to rattle, dragged all over the floor. So, they got up, lit the lamp—it was a farmhouse, no electricity. They lit the light, and there was not a thing out of place, so they went back to bed. About the time they laid down, the door blew open. He got up and shut the door. It blew open again. He got up and he shut it again. He went back to bed, and his wife said "I'm gettin' outa here. I ain't stayin' here."

He said, "Why, there's nothing wrong. I'll get it."

She said, "How you gonna stop it?"

He got out of bed, outside to the shop, got a brace and bit, bored a hole through the wall, a hole through the door, put him a chain in there and put a padlock on it. "Now," he said, "go back to bed. It can't open."

Crash, bang, up come the door. He got up and looked. The chain was not broken; the holes were not torn out, but the lock was still on the door standing wide open. So it was about four in the morning by the time it had all happened, and they left and walked about four miles to my brother-in-law's house. When they knocked on the door he said, "What's the matter?"

"We've come to stay all night with you. We'll never go back in that house again." He said, "We see why no one will rent it, cause it *is* haunted." They left crops and all and never went back.

The persistence of this tale and hundreds like it suggests appreciation for the Gothic touch. The role of belief in keeping such tales in circulation is impossible to evaluate accurately. No one will deny that some people believe profoundly in the supernatural events they relate, yet putting them in the first person or recounting fairly standard motifs as experiences of friends or family is the manipulation mentioned above: making a good story better or more believable, or, in the case of ghost tales, more effectively scary.

In Russellville, the story goes, is a little house with a

dormer window which sometimes shows the clear image of a young woman as though it has been etched into the glass. It is the image of a girl who was putting on her best dress to attend a very important party. As she prepared for the event she was aware of a brewing storm, and she prayed for good weather so that the good dress and the party would not be spoiled. But the crashing thunderstorm came anyway. Enraged, the girl shook her fist at the sky and cursed God. Immediately, a bolt of lightning struck the house, killing the blasphemer and etching her image in the glass of the window. It appears only on certain cloudy days. Owners have tried to cover it by painting over the glass, but the image shows through the paint. One version of the story has it that owners have even removed the ghostly windowpane and replaced it, but the image returns to the site in the new glass.

The idea of cosmic retribution is an old one. So is the idea of a persistent image or bloodstain. The most interesting feature of this folktale is the fact that it has parallel versions for other communities in Kentucky and even out of the state. D. K. Wilgus assembled a number of variants of this tale for discussion in *Western Folklore* in 1970. More recently one old-time riverman recalled a similar tale he had picked up on the river many years ago. In this instance the victim was an old man with a long beard who was sitting in a rocking chair at an Owensboro hotel when a lightning bolt struck and killed him. Onlookers found his image etched in the windowpane so clearly that it looked like an old-fashioned glass photograph negative. A local photographer removed the windowpane, the old riverman said, and made a good photographic print from it!

When a folklorist encounters a "belief" tale with this much particular detail he is rightly wary. Part of the tradition of telling tall tales is to render them with a straight face, to solemnly aver that they are true, and to support that assertion with specific local particulars.

This tradition mingles with the well established technique of gulling the listener into taking the tale seriously, then pulling the rug out with a punch line at the end. Consider the Earl Thomas rendition of a ghost tale:

When I was young and still living at home, my father had lots of land down along the Barren River. He had twelve tenant houses on that land, and all of them stayed occupied except one. It had stood empty so long it was falling into decay.

One day I asked my father about that particular house. I said, "Father, how come nobody ever lives in that old house?"

He said, "Well, it stands over there by that old graveyard, you know. Some says it's hanted."

I didn't believe much in hants, and I said to myself I would just go over there some night and see for myself. Sure enough, shortly after that it was a clear evening, and I had nothing else to do, so I took a lantern and went over there shortly before sundown. I looked the place over good. Nothing there but a few old boxes. I took a box out on the porch to sit on, set one up in the front room for my lantern, and when it began to get dark, I lit my lantern. Then I went out on the porch to sit down and see what I could see.

Just a little while after it got dark, the lantern went out. I figured maybe it was only a draft in the house, so I went back in and lit it again. Then I went back by my box to sit and wait. I hadn't been sitting there more than five minutes, I guess, when my lantern went out again. This time it made me a little bit nervous because I was sure I didn't feel any draft, but I went in and lit the lantern again. Said, "I'll light you this time, but if you go out again, I'm gone."

Well, I went back out on the porch and sat down. Looked back at the door, and there stood this great big outline of a man. Couldn't see his features, but he was big. He said, "We're by ourselves tonight, aren't we?"

I said, "Yes, but not for long."

I jumped off that porch and hit the ground running. I ran as hard as I could across the pasture field, a half a mile, I guess. Finally, I was so out of breath, I had to stop. There I was, sitting on a log, panting, when I could feel someone beside me.

He said, "We had a pretty good race, didn't we?"

I said, "Yes, and we're going to have another." I lit out again, and I guess I kicked up so much dust between there and home he couldn't keep up. I didn't see him again.

Notice that this narrator went a sentence too far, past his punch line. Another "ghost" tale is similar in that the point of the telling is in the humor rather than in real or pretended belief in ghosts:

When I was about eight years old, I lived down at Celina. There was a creek there that ran through the farmland, and it had a good deep place that everybody around there used for a swimming hole. In this swimming hole, at one end, there was this tree that had fell down over the water, and the log was handy to sit on or dive off of into the water.

Well, a girl that was swimming there got drownded. Some time after that, folks started seeing that girl sitting out there on the end of the log. Some believed it, and some didn't. Finally, a bunch of people, growed up and younguns alike, decided to go out there of an evening to see if they could see the spirit of that drownded girl.

One feller in the neighborhood was quite a joker. He stuttered something awful, and he was always up to something. He decided to make sure that the other people would see something, so he got out there ahead of the rest, wrapped himself up in a sheet, and sat down on the end of the log.

Pretty soon, here come the crowd of curious folks. As soon as they come up to the bank, one man hollered out, "There she is, right on the end."

Then another feller hollered, real excited, "Look, *two* of 'em on the log."

Well, that joker on the log heard that, and he jumped right off into the water. Scared the people on the bank so much they took off running. He come up spluttering and hollering, "W-w-wait f-f-fer mmmm-me." They all ran faster, and he come up behind, trying to catch up, still hollering, "W-w-wait f-f-fer mmmm-me."

I could never decide if there really was two of 'em on the log or not. Or who played a joke on who.

Another kind of folk telling which often involves an element of belief is the place-name legend. A colorful place name, especially, is likely to have an explanation of its origin, sometimes several explanations. These brief and often humorous tales are great favorites of journalistic writers whose space is limited and who need a flow of anecdotal material. Allan Trout maintained his "Greetings" column in the *Courier-Journal* for many years on such fare, and Joe Creason ably carried on the tradition until his death in 1974.

The title "Place Name Stories of Kentucky Waterways and Ponds, with a Note on Bottomless Pools" by Herbert Halpert in the 1961 *Kentucky Folklore Record* contains within itself the suggestion that place-name legends may be systematically collected and categorized. A portion of Halpert's introductory note presents the function of material of this kind:

The making and telling of place name stories to explain names given by an older generation is such a vital part of our folktale tradition that one is led to ask what basic needs it satisfies. The simplest function of these place name legends is probably that of satisfying the natural curiosity of those who follow the namers about how and why certain local names were given. In a less obvious way the explanations serve as a part of folk history—the body of traditional lore which gives any group its feeling of continuity with their forebears on the land. The sense of belonging to a certain area or home place is certainly strengthened by this kind of documentation, whether the stories are historically true or not. Some of the stories about creeks and ponds have an additional function as bogey tales meant to keep children from playing dangerously near the water.

Halpert follows these comments with texts of short narratives about streams, ponds, and sinks in western Kentucky. Four of these ostensibly explain the origin of the name for Panther Creek. In version A the new sprouts on an old sycamore tree are presumably the result of a panther clawing the trunk of the tree; in version B two men out hunting were attracted to the spot by a panther's screams; in version C a Negro crossing the stream in pioneer days shot a panther on a tree limb overhanging the creek; and in version D a settler saw the eyes of a big cat through the brush as he forded the stream, shot at them, and found that he had killed a huge black panther. All of these locally collected narratives refer to the same place name.

It is apparent that local details of Kentucky folk history and legendry come to light only through local inquiry. In Kentucky the opportunities seem endless. *A Guide to Kentucky Place Names* by Thomas P. Field (Kentucky Geological Survey, 1961) is a compact gazetteer of place names deriving from topographical maps and attendant materials. It lists alphabetically 39,212 place names in Kentucky, only 6,500 of which are populated places and rural neighborhoods.

Cursory examination of this listing gives some impression of pioneer Kentucky. Beginning with one of the examples mentioned above, one finds twenty-seven "Panther" entries, including creeks, branches, schools, and licks. It would appear that the panther made an impression on the minds of the people who gave the names. More important would be names associated with life-sustaining creatures—deer and turkey. The listings for "Deer" and its derivatives add up to twenty-nine. The more colorful "Buck" was much more widely used: twenty-eight "Buck Branch" names, thirty-three "Buck Creek" names, and forty-four others such as licks and knobs, all adding up to more than one hundred "Buck" associated names of places. "Turkey" derivatives total about the same.

But this is not all. Field's names were listed from the official topographic maps. Anyone who asks for directions in a rural neighborhood will discover that there are rocks, branches, and hollows known by local names but which are not listed or mapped in any official way.

Obviously, no single person could find the time to make local inquiries about place names and their historical or legendary derivation over the whole state. Such a project requires the spare-time interest of a person or group able to interest others over the state who have access to community or county informants. Kentucky has such an organization.

Robert M. Rennick, at Prestonburg, is coordinator of the Kentucky Section, Place Name Survey of the United States. In a brief handbook prepared for volunteer contributors Rennick notes:

We often come across names that defy all attempts at explanation. For this reason they may have inspired stories or legends that local residents or others offer to account for them (e.g. Helechawa, Whoopflarea). These are actually ex-post-facto accounts, invented to explain a name that defies explanation but are usually accepted by local residents and circulated with great sincerity. An investigator is also likely to find many of these popular accounts given for names that otherwise have been verified.

The story of Sally's Rock illustrates what Rennick means by ex-post-facto accounts. Sally's Rock is located at the confluence of the Barren and Gasper rivers in Warren County. The place was named for Sally Beck, a colorful character who used to stand on a pinnacle high above the river and hail packet boats through a megaphone. Both Sally and the rock are now gone, but the name is well established and clearly labeled on topographic maps. Because the spot high above the river affords an excellent panoramic view, it was once a popular place for young people to congregate, as is evidenced by the many initials scratched into the friable rock along the edge of the cliff. These are the initials of people who knew the place a generation or two ago, before it became less accessible because of ownership, fences, and gates.

The high school crowd still drives along the river to "Sally's Rock" to park, but the parkers are not aware that they have transferred the name to a new location. Neither are they aware of the original source of the name. Some have invented a new tale about a properly romantic Sally who hurled herself from the heights when disappointed in love.

Such a metamorphosis doesn't yield much in the way of history, but it does tell something about people.

6

KENTUCKY SINGERS

E VERY YEAR thousands of school children read a few ballads in their literature textbooks. "Sir Patrick Spens," "Edward," and "Get Up and Bar the Door" appear regularly as specimens of poetry, sometimes clearly identified as songs, sometimes not. Often a student who has seen the selections in a literature textbook goes on through life thinking of them as rather quaint poems, like Robert Frost's "Mending Wall" in a peculiar dialect.

> *It fell about the Martinmas time,*
> *And a gay time it was then,*
> *When our good wife got puddings to make,*
> *And she's boiled them in a pan.*

This is part of the heritage of literature and language emphasis deriving from Child, Kittredge, and their students. They were interested in literature and language, but they did not quite know how to handle music.

When Josiah Combs's settlement school teacher sent the first batch of his authentic Kentucky mountain ballads to the *Journal of American Folklore*, Kittredge published them with notes like this:

This version of "Lord Thomas and Fair Annet" (Child, No. 73) should be compared with the Virginian copy communicated to the Folk-Lore Journal by Mr. W. H. Babcock (vii, 33) and printed by Child, iii, 509. A few readings from another version furnished by Miss Pettit are given in footnotes (marked B).

1. *"Mother O mother, go riddle my sport;*
    Go riddle it all as one:
    Must I go marry fair Alender,
    Or bring the brown girl home?"

2. *"The brown girl she has house and land,*
    Fair Alender has none;
    Therefore I warn you as a blessing,
    Go bring the brown girl home."

One sees that Kittredge expresses no interest in the singer and his music. His attention is directed to the words only, along with the words of comparative texts. It would be an error, however, to think of all these scholars as ignorant of tunes. Even Combs, a singer of ballads, tended to adopt a literary emphasis after he joined the ranks of the scholars. The greatest impediment to collection and study of whole songs was simply the lack of a practical portable recording device. The only other way to collect whole songs (text and tune) was by note pad and pencil, but this required extensive musical training, an accurate ear for notation of tunes, and, above all, strong enough motivation to clamber up creek beds and across footlogs to get to the best singers. Not until 1916 did that happy combination fall into place.

Like the irony of Combs's study of Southern folksong first appearing abroad in French, it was a visiting English music teacher who learned almost accidentally about Appalachian songs and set out to collect them. Cecil Sharp had collected folk songs and dances in England prior to World War I. He had developed great enthusiasm for folk dance revival, but this movement had stalled in England because of the war. Needing money, he agreed to come to the United States to assist Granville Barker in a New York production of *A Midsummer Night's Dream*. He stayed on to give folk dance lectures and lessons, and it was during a brief respite from these lectures brought on by illness that Mrs. Olive Dame Campbell caught up with him.

Mrs. Campbell had traveled through the southern highlands with her husband, John C. Campbell, author of *The Southern Highlander and His Homeland* (1921). Lacking necessary training for song collection, she had nevertheless been so attracted to mountain singing that she had collected about seventy songs. When she showed her manuscripts to Sharp in 1915 he suddenly realized that in the United States was a pocket of tradition richer than anything he had encountered in England. He projected a collection tour for the following year.

Starting from Mrs. Campbell's home in Asheville, North Carolina, Cecil Sharp and his tireless co-worker and biographer, Maud Karpeles, began a richly rewarding collecting tour through the southern Appalachians. It should be stressed that this collection was Appalachian rather than confined to Kentucky. The Kentucky period of Sharp's collecting did occur, however, in the fall of 1917. In all, he spent parts of 1916, 1917, and 1918 collecting mountain songs. Summing up his accomplishments, Karpeles wrote:

> It would seem that Cecil Sharp had every reason to be satisfied. He had collected from 281 singers a total of 1,612 tunes, including variants, representing about 500 different songs and ballads. . . .
>
> From the scientific standpoint the value of the collection lies in the fact that it is an expression of the innate musical culture of a homogeneous community. To Cecil Sharp the mountain community was an outstanding example of "the supreme cultural value of an inherited tradition."

One of the many interesting responses to Sharp's collecting was the respect and interest shown by American scholars, most of whom had been busily engaged in collecting texts without tunes. Even Kittredge begged a copy of Sharp's manuscript to be deposited at the Harvard library.

Sharp died in England in 1924. The fruits of the combined efforts of Sharp, Olive Dame Campbell, and Maud Karpeles appeared in *English Folk Songs from the Southern Appalachians,* edited by Maud Karpeles in two volumes, 1932. This stands as the most representative collection of mountain songs and tunes in that no subsequent collector has had or could have access to the isolated culture that was already rapidly changing even in Sharp's time. Recognizing this, Sharp wrote in a letter to University of Virginia Professor Alphonso Smith, "In Kentucky the tradition was, I imagine, in full blast up to a few years ago, and still is in some of the most remote districts, but is now being rapidly killed in its prime by industrialism. In Kentucky it is a case of sudden death; in Virginia of euthanasia."

Another indication of displacement of old English ballads by popular and gospel music is Maud Karpeles's observation, "The whole time we were in the mountains we never heard a poor tune (except sometimes at the missionary settlements, or on the rare occasions when we stayed at a summer resort hotel) and nearly all were of surpassing beauty."

In August 1917, Sharp visited Pine Mountain Settlement School, then accessible only by walking over a steep mountain trail. Here he met Evelyn Kendrick Wells, who promptly directed him to singers she had already been collecting from. She was secretary and acting director of the school from 1915 to 1928, and after that went on to complete a distinguished career as an English professor at Wellesley College. Miss Wells, like Miss Pettit, had been actively interested in the mountain ballad tradition. Her friendship with Maud Karpeles continued through the years to 1955, when the two women, this time with a tape recorder, tried retracing some of the collecting jaunts of 1917, only to prove Sharp's point made earlier, that the singing tradition was breaking up. Of the 1955 collecting tour with Evelyn Wells, Karpeles remarks, "The region is no longer a folksong collector's paradise, for the serpent, in the form of the radio, has crept in, bearing its insidious hill-billy and other 'pop' songs."

Evelyn Wells never lost her interest in Kentucky folklore, and her interest, specifically in the ballad, led to research and collecting which ultimately bore fruit in a college textbook, already a classic in the field: *The Ballad Tree* (1950). This is a book which pays full measure of attention to both texts and tunes as it develops the history and literary associations of the ballad in the English-speaking world. It also draws heavily on Miss Wells's Kentucky experience. A letter from her to the editor of *Kentucky Folklore Record* in 1973 attested to her continuing interest, and it may also mark a record for the time span of personal involvement.

Intensive collection and study of Old-World balladry in America during the first half of the twentieth century shed a great deal of light on the way oral traditions persist, adapt to changing times, and function in the community. Since this aspect of the singing tradition was already diminishing early in the century, it gradually became more and more apparent that emphasis exclusively on English and Scottish ballads was somewhat analogous to pumping on a dry well. If Kentucky has a continuing singing tradition, it must reflect the authentic lifestyle of Kentucky folk.

The shift of emphasis in collection and study became apparent with the renaissance of the Kentucky Folklore Society, sparked by the arrival of D. K. Wilgus at Western Kentucky University in 1950. Wilgus was working on his doctoral dissertation when he arrived in Bowling Green. It was later published by Rutgers University Press (1959) as *Anglo-American Folksong Scholarship since 1898*. The title is significant in that 1898 was the date of the publication of Child's *English and Scottish Popular Ballads,* the monumental work that had dominated folksong thought during the first half of the century. Among the other accomplishments in Wilgus's study was a declaration of independence from the Child domination over scholarship.

In one chapter Wilgus joined forces with John Greenway, whose *American Folksongs of Protest* (1953) had created a stir in academic circles by its suggestion that solidarity songs of union workers were folksongs. Greenway's aggressive position was that the American workers (real *folk*) had no business being preoccupied with lords and ladies in castles and bowers; their proper concerns were expressed in such songs as "Down on the Picket Line" and "Dump the Bosses off Your Back." Greenway also suggested that the identity of the composer and the nature of the content were more important than long persistence in history as criteria for identification of folksong. Thus to him, "The Kentucky Miner's Dreadful Fight" became a folksong the minute Aunt Molly Jackson scribbled it on a piece of paper.

Wilgus accepted these ideas and pushed even further to consideration of early phonograph recordings as authentic folksong documents. In doing so, he pioneered in viewing so-called hillbilly music as a valid modern manifestation of folksong—a blending of older elements of content and style with contemporary culture.

With the folksong field thus redefined, Wilgus began an energetic decade of collection, ably supported by Gordon Wilson, his department head, and by the other folklorists strategically located across the state: Herbert Halpert at Murray, William Hugh Jansen at Lexington, and George Boswell at Morehead. This movement had additional impetus from the continuing work of Cratis Williams at Appalachian State University. Williams's master's thesis, "Ballads and Songs," had been completed at the University of Kentucky in 1937, and he continues to this day with scholarship, lectures, and public singing performances which display a versatility reminiscent of that of Josiah Combs.

As the Western Kentucky Folklore Archive grew, Wilgus was able to present authority rather than guesswork for the status of Kentucky folksong, and although he was practically hooted down when he first proposed a regular review section for phonograph recordings in the staid *Journal of American Folklore,* this feature has since become a standard item in this and other folklore journals. The accumulation of rare early phonograph recordings, old song-ballet books (hand-written notebooks of song texts prized by old-time singers), and field-collected texts continues to reveal survivals, recombinations, and strands of associated tradition not understood or even suspected at an earlier time.

An illustration is "Ten Broeck and Mollie: A Race and a Ballad," written for *Kentucky Folklore Record* by Wilgus in 1956. His article concerns some puzzling field-collected fragments of song about the famous 1878 horse race which is also the subject of a poem quoted in *All That's Kentucky.* In bringing together his information Wilgus quoted a portion of a song provided by E. C. Perrow:

> *Way up in de mountain whah Ten Brook wuz bo'n*
> *De people all said dat he come dah in a sto'm.*
>
> *Ten Brook he made it in two-twenty-three;*
> *Gon' to hab it published in de new Galilee!*
>
> *Harper bet silber; de Californians bet gol';*
> *Ten Brook beat Molly to a hole in de wall.*

Wilgus then notes that Jean Thomas, in *Ballad Makin' in the Mountains of Kentucky* (1939), had reported fragments from eastern Kentucky. The most complete version with music is on a Bill Monroe phonograph recording, a version that varies somewhat from the Grand Old Opry Song Folio. Wilgus also reports a Stanley Brothers recording, other collectors' reports of fragments or variants of the song, and magazine articles, to develop the background. When he gets to the Library of Congress, Music Division, Archive of American Folksong, he finds this combination:

> *Old Kimball was a gray nag, old Nellie was a*
> *   brown;*
> *Old Kimball beat old Nellie on the very first*
> *   go-round.*
>
> *And I see, and I see, and I see,*
> *On the fourth day of July.*

The stanza is, of course, a mutation of the Perrow 1909 text, "Skewball" becoming "Kimball," and "Molly" becoming "Nellie." But the variant preserves not only the "very first go-round"—a clear reference to the Louisville race—but a refrain which recalls the day of the race. As the remaining stanzas are non-diagnostic, we are unable to identify this text as either "Skew Ball" or "Ten Broeck," unless we simply use the name as diagnostic.

Essentially, what Wilgus showed was that an old Irish broadside ballad about a horse race (with talking horses) had converged with the ballad report of the Louisville horse race. The Irish "Skew Ball" had changed to "Stewball" in American Negro worksong versions. More was to come. In the following issue of the *Record*, Wilgus announced two more fragments collected by Herbert Halpert. In one,

> *Tinpenny and Mollie were off for the green;*
> *Tinpenny and Mollie were sights to be seen.*

In the other,

> *Ten Brook he's an old gray horse an' Mollie*
> *   she's a roan.*

> Ten Brooks he brought silver and Mollie she
> brought gold.

Still later Jansen reported for the *Record* yet another fragment recorded by Mrs. Evelyn Polk Eldred of Princeton, Kentucky:

> *Oh, the day was fer racing and Tin Brook*
> *to run,*
> *The hosses came marching in like prisoners*
> *to be hung;*
> *The bell it did tap and the flag it did*
> *fall,*
> *And Mollie went a-darting for the hole in*
> *the wall.*
> CHORUS: *You'd better run, Mollie, run,*
> *Run, Mollie, run.*

Jansen points out lines in this version which seem to associate it with black-face minstrelsy. All the influences and convergences are not yet clear. No original composer or date of composition has been established.

In 1970, Jean Thomason (a fifth-generation folklorist in that she had completed her master's degree at Western Kentucky University) published a full text of "Ten Broeck and Mollie" that she had collected from Jesse Blair in Grayson County:

> *Molly said to old Tinbrook*
> *Before dat race was run*
> *Take me to the stables*
> *And tell 'em feed me some*
> *Tell 'em feed me some, Oh Lord,*
> *Tell 'em feed me some.*
>
> *Tinbrooks was a big bay hoss*
> *A great long shaggy mane*
> *Take him down to Old Memphus*
> *And he c'n outrun the train*
> *He'll outrun the train, Oh Lord,*
> *And he'll outrun the train.*

Blair had learned the song in 1898, but he had also heard the Bill Monroe version on a phonograph record more recently. Mrs. Thomason's review of the problem does not answer all the questions about Ten Broeck and his progeny in poetry and song. However, it does illustrate with a single vivid example the value of continuing collection and a good archiving system which will permit ready access to manuscript and tape-recorded materials. Considered singly, any one of the fragments or versions mentioned above is relatively meaningless—a scrap of an unimportant and mostly forgotten old song about a horse race. Quite another response occurs when one examines the whole cluster. Vistas of folk history and folk art open up. One is reminded of the song-making tradition in Black America, where borrowed and misunderstood "Skew" becomes familiar and desirable "Stew." The song is no longer Irish. Questions arise. Did a black trainer who knew "Stewball" compose a song about Ten Broeck? Is there a lost original about Ten Broeck which became confused with another song in ever-recombining oral transmission? Inevitably one observes that the folk reflect events important to them in their oral literature, and what could be more natural in Kentucky than to memorialize a horse race?

If John Greenway was right in his feeling that modern folk have more business singing about modern working conditions than about lords and ladies, then some evidence of this should be reflected in modern collection. The Kentucky coalfields provide one good illustration of the fact that people's songs do spring out of a modern industrial environment. The text of one of Aunt Molly Jackson's songs appeared in a 1961 issue of *Kentucky Folklore Record.*

KENTUCKY MINERS' HUNGRY BLUES

I am sad and wearied, I have got the hungry ragged blues,

Not a penny in my pocket to buy one thing
    I need to use.
I was up this morning with the worst blues
    I ever had in my life,
Not a bit to cook for breakfast, or for a
    coal miner's wife.

When my husband works in the coal mines, he
    loads a car on every trip.
When he goes to the office that evenin' and
    gits denied of scrip
Just because it took all he had made that
    day to pay his mine expense.
Just because it took all he had made that
    day to pay his mine expense.
A man that will just work for coal, light
    and carbide, he got a speck of sense.

The poor women in this coal camp are a
    sitt' with bowed down heads,
Ragged and barefooted and their children
    a-cryin' for bread.
No food, no clothes for our children
    I am sure this ain't no lie.
If we caint get no more for our labor, we
    will starve to death and die.

Please don't go under those mountains, with
    the slate hanging over your head,
Please don't go under those mountains, with
    the slate hanging over your head,
And work for just coal, light and carbide
    and your children a crying out for bread.
I pray you take my counsel, please take a
    friend's advice.
Don't load no more, don't put out no more
    till you can get a living price.

This minin' town I live in is a sad and a
    lonely place,
This minin' town I live in is a sad and a
    lonely place,

> Where pity and starvation is pictured in
>   every face.
> Everybody hungry and ragged, no slippers
>   on their feet,
> Everybody hungry and ragged, no slippers
>   on their feet,
> All a-going 'round from place to place a
>   bummin' a bite to eat.
> Listen my friends and comrades, please take
>   a friend's advice,
> Don't load no more of this dirty coal until
>   you get a livin' price.

This issue of the *Record* was exclusively devoted to the memory of Aunt Molly Jackson (Mary Magdalene Garland Stewart Jackson Stamos, 1880–1960). The song is one of many she composed in Harlan County during the bad days of the early 1930s. In his contribution to the memorial issue John Greenway wrote of her, "Folklorists gravitated to Aunt Molly like iron filings to a magnet," and then went on to recall both his frustration and his gratification derived from working with her.

Alan Lomax wrote in the same issue:

Aunt Molly Jackson and Texas Gladden were the finest traditional singers I met in the United States. Aunt Molly's style of singing marks a peak of the wild, strident, highly emotional manner of eastern Kentucky. Her texts and especially her tunes are magnificent. . . .

She was a tigress, a great talker and a great bard. Her songs of protest can only be matched by those of Woody Guthrie, but they were more passionate than his, and they cut deeper.

The coalfields of Kentucky, then, regarded as a destructive intrusion by Cecil Sharp, who sought inherited English song, have produced a singing tradition of their own. A phonograph recording produced by the Music Division of the Library of Congress entitled "Songs and Ballads of the Bituminous Miners" (AFS L60) is another indication. It contains three selections from Kentucky: "That Little Lump of Coal" sung by William March and Richard Lawson at Kenvir, "Harlan County Blues" sung by George Davis at Glomawr, and "Hignite Blues" sung by Wesley J. Turner at Shamrock Mountain.

A folksong topic of perennial interest is murder, especially murdered girls. Although the theme is ancient, enough girls are actually murdered to provide specific new situations for the folk bards. Through the years a number of murdered-girl ballads have appeared in the *Record*. Virgil Sturgill contributed a text of "The Murder of Lottie Yates" in 1959:

> *Come listen, friends, while I relate*
> *Of a Crime committed in Kentucky State.*
> *It was the murder of poor Lottie Yates,*
> *I hope she's passed through Heaven's gates.*
>
> *It was a night in the month of May*
> *While she in bed with her baby lay,*
> *The dirk was hurled with a wicked dart*
> *That caused poor Lottie and her babe to part.*
>
> . . . .
>
> *They placed the culprit on the verge,*
> *No funeral song nor lonesome dirge,*
> *With none to sing but the nightingale*
> *To mourn his loss or his sad bewail.*
>
> *The time has come; he must make the leap*
> *While frantic shadows o'er him creep.*
> *He's gone; he's swung beneath the sky.*
> *For a cruel murder he had to die.*
>
> *This ends these lines of which we read*
> *Of a crime so black with its bloody deed,*
> *May all mankind who marry a wife*
> *Live true and faithful all their life.*

That same year Cratis Williams provided two texts of "Stella Kenney," ballads about a girl murdered near Olive Hill.

1. *It was on a Sunday night*
   The second day of May,
   Stella Kenney was murdered
   (While) for home she was on her way.

6. *There was her dear old father*
   A-kneeling by her side;
   "With seven gashes on her head,
   No wonder Stella died."

15. *Now Stella's gone to heaven,*
    In that bright world so fair;
    Where there, the Bible tells us,
    Will be no murder there.

Other murdered girls are celebrated in Kentucky song, along with their topical kin, feuders and outlaws. The murdered-girl complex is selected here to illustrate once more the insights to be gained from adequate archival holdings.

In 1973 the American Folklore Society published in its Memoir Series, edited by William Hugh Jansen, *Poor Pearl, Poor Girl* by Anne B. Cohen. The book title is a quotation of one line of one version of a Kentucky murder ballad generally known as "Pearl Bryan."

The event memorialized in song was the decapitation murder of an Indiana girl, Pearl Bryan, on February 1, 1896. One folksong report goes like this:

Now ladies, if you listen
A story I'll relate
That happened near Fort Thomas
In old Kentucky State

'Twas late in January
This awful deed was done
By Jackson and by Walling
How cold their blood did run

How bold these cruel villains
To do this awful deed

To hide away Pearl Bryan
When she to them did plead.

Because of the grisly nature of the crime (the head of the victim was never found!) both journalists and folk bards reported it repeatedly and variously. The long, headline-making trial of the two men accused of the murder provided specific phrases and images which could be worked into song, and the clichés of folk balladry set up stereotypes for newspaper reporters. Tracing the songs through the years, Anne Cohen found such distinctly different texts among the 135 she examined that she classified them as Pearl Bryan I, II, III, IV, V, and VI, Unclassifiable, and Non-Traditional. Even this dividing up did not categorize adequately, for she found it necessary to divide "Pearl Bryan I" into "A. Dalhart Group, B. Non-Dalhart Group, C. Dalhart-Non-Dalhart Mixture, and D. Mixed Texts of Pearl Bryan I." She examined manuscripts, published collections, sheet music, and phonograph recordings, including forty-five items from the Western Kentucky Folklore Archive.

The book was originally a master's thesis done under the direction of D. K. Wilgus. If it were merely an exercise in establishing the major variant texts that have developed from a single sensational event, it would contribute little to knowledge. It does much more than that. The ballad texts are analyzed in conjunction with newspaper accounts of the time to bring out a closely woven, well documented exposition of stereotypes in popular culture. These affected journalistic responses to the event and possibly affected the course of justice. In addition to being a study of the ballad muse, then, Cohen's study contributes to knowledge of history and popular psychology.

Extended studies similar in scope to Cohen's treatment of "Pearl Bryan" await the attention of scholars. One or more of these should focus on modern gospel singing groups. The phenomenon is contemporary, but content and performance style are clearly projections of earlier traditions. Another is the role of folk elements in modern country-western music. The subject has already received some attention from specialists, but, complicated as it is by media and promotion in contemporary popular culture, much yet waits to be done. Still another subject not fully explored is the role of song in the lives of displaced Kentuckians who have migrated to northern industrial centers. These people sometimes maintain a group identity by sharing their folk traditions.

These examples have stressed the academic environment, yet academic people would have little to work with were it not for the friendly cooperation of people in all walks of life. It is they who respond to language questionnaires, sing their songs, and tell stories to inquiring collectors. Theirs is the reservoir of traditional thought and expression which was recognized and utilized by field workers for the earliest enterprise of a beginning recording industry and programming for early radio broadcasting. In many instances the popular entertainment people were on the scene ahead of the academicians.

Recognition and appreciation of folksong by the general public depends on the skills of nonacademic performers, people like Jean Thomas, John Jacob Niles, and Jean Ritchie. Not only have these and many others written and performed for the public; they have also been tireless field workers, collecting materials for their various enterprises.

In *Ballad Makin' in the Mountains of Kentucky,* Jean Thomas stresses the art of folk composition. "Year after year in my travels through the mountains of Kentucky, on one mission or another, I 'set down' all sorts of ballads and tunes, many of which the mountain minstrel, or his 'own blood kin,' claimed to have 'made up right out of his head.'" Her collection is impressive—ballads about feuds, war, killings, and other mountain subjects interspersed with vividly recalled conversations with the singers and their families.

Jean Thomas stresses the antique and quaint, yet, for the 1930s, her view was remarkably clear. In the closing chapter, "Progress," she states, "The art of ballad making is not lost in the mountains of Kentucky but has changed—with the times. . . . Progress stalks the hills like a giant, stamping its imprint everywhere, even upon the craft of ballad making." She follows by quoting a modern ballad about the Tennessee Valley Authority.

People who have never heard of the Kentucky Folklore Society or any of its members have heard of Jean Thomas. In 1935, certainly well before any hint of the folksong revival, she had successfully supervised the assembly of a "folk opera" for radio broadcast. Her "Wee House in the Wood" at Ashland became known to the world as the site of pioneering folk festivals.

John Jacob Niles of Winchester is the grand old man of Kentucky folksong on the concert stage. By his own account, he was among the first collectors of Kentucky song. In the introduction to his *The Ballad Book of John Jacob Niles* he recalls,

By the time I was 20 years of age (1912) well-informed scholars in Virginia, West Virginia, and North Carolina were collecting folklore, but I knew nothing of this. . . .

So for many years my collection was a private family property, out of which I was selecting . . . for concert and lecture appearances.

Niles has had a long and rewarding career as a performing artist, writer, and composer. His impressive bibliography of copyrighted sheet music attests to his technical skill, and his concert performance career attests to his skill in dramatic presentation. His typical accompaniment instrument is an oversize dulcimer of his own design. His is what one modern scholar calls the "aesthetic projection" of folksong.

Jean Ritchie, in her engaging biography *Singing Family of the Cumberlands* (1955), details the remarkable performance abilities of the Balis Ritchie family of Viper, Kentucky. Born the youngest of fifteen children in 1922, Jean was the most likely of the "younguns" to observe and chronicle the transition from mountain isolation to the modern era of mobility and mass media.

From family tradition rather than personal observation she tells of the opening settlement schools: "On a day in the late spring of 1895 a strange woman drove into Hazard in a wagon, said she had come all the way from Lexington down in the Blue Grass country. . . . Her name was Katherine Pettit and folks couldn't rightly make out why she had come all that weary way up into Perry County, she had no people here that anyone could see." Her account of the gradual development of the settlement schools shifts finally to Pine Mountain: "Well, when Miss Pettit got the school to running smooth, she went to Pine Mountain in Harlan County where they had been begging her to come and start up a school. In 1913 she began work on the Pine Mountain Settlement School. If you go down there right now, anyone will tell you that these are two of the finest schools to be found anywhere in the Kentucky Mountains."

Singing Family of the Cumberlands is intimate, joyous, and liberally sprinkled with the songs and other pastimes of aunts, uncles, parents, and siblings. The entertainment was vital, home-made. The account of the "serpent," as Maud Karpeles characterized the radio, is illuminating. When the Ritchie family acquired a radio it was of the early headphones type. Only one person could listen at a time. In such a large family a scramble ensued. For the first time the Ritchies were hearing "hillbilly" music on mass media—"Pale Wildwood Flower," "Zeb Turney's Girl," and "Sweet Fern." Jean discovered that singing "Barbry Ellen" was shamefully old fashioned. "Hillbilly songs, the radio called the music, and it claimed that these songs were sung all through the mountains, but we never had heard anything just like them before. I guess if it hadn't been for the radio it's no telling how long it would have taken us to find out that we were hillbillies, or what kind of songs we were supposed to sing."

Jean Ritchie chose the old songs and the old style for her performance career. A folk festival in Kentucky seems hardly complete without her appearance. Writing, composing, arranging, she continues to draw on her impeccably traditional background.

Many other Kentuckians contribute to the aesthetic projection of regional folk arts, both as singers and organizers of public performance. Buell Kazee, Yvonne Gregory, Bradley Kinkaid, Edna Ritchie, and Bill Monroe come immediately to mind. Sarah Gertrude Knott of Paducah has worked tirelessly to project old-time arts into public performance.

In 1973, the threshold of Kentucky's bicentennial year, the Festival of American Folklife in Washington, D. C., sponsored by the Smithsonian Institution, featured traditional Kentucky. In the music section, fiddlers, banjo players, gospel singers, and blue grass bands mingled with demonstrations of material culture such as broom making and tobacco twisting. If the Ritchie family wanted to meet their performing friends at a convention, that was the place.

Occasionally one hears a scholar speaking critically of concert or festival performance as not being "authentic." The response to this is that a song buried in the archives or printed in a scholarly journal is not "authentic" either. Oral traditions are a product and possession of all the folk, and they are used in different ways, for study by some, for entertainment by others, and this is the way it should be. A good performer must necessarily use costume, props, and a sense of the dramatic if he is to succeed. Folklorists, in spite of preoccupation with texts and archives, generally approve of these aesthetic projections, for they are also aware of the way art and literature feed on folk sources.

7

FOLKLORE IN KENTUCKY LITERATURE

> Aunt Ailsie first heard the news from her son's wife, Ruthena, who, returning from a trading trip to The Forks, reined in her nag to call,—
>
> "Maw, there's a passel of quare women come in from furrin parts and sot 'em up some cloth houses there on the p'int above the courthouse, and carrying on some of the outlandishest doings ever you heard of."

JEAN RITCHIE'S account of the arrival of settlement school teachers echoes these beginning lines of *The Quare Women* by Lucy Furman. The book is a romance created in the historical setting of the settlement school period. It was an immediate success following its first printing in 1923. Furman's use of authentic Kentucky mountain folklore continues to be an interesting aspect of a novel which is otherwise too quaintly sentimental for most modern tastes. The folkloristic content ranges through the various categories: language, folk history and legend, song, beliefs and practices.

One can abstract a lexicon of regional dialect from *The Quare Women*. Passel, quare, furrin, plumb proper, fotched, seed (saw), narry grain (none), holped, hairth (hearth), clifts, and pineblank (straight at) occur in a half-dozen pages; this promise of a rather full exposition of colorful regional speech is fulfilled in the remainder of the book.

The dialect carries over into song texts, which occur naturally in the development of character and events.

> Lady Isabel in her bower a-sewing,
>   All as the gowans grow gay,
> Then she hears an Elf Knight his horn a-blowing,
>   The first morning in May.

The stern old tradition of mountain feuds works naturally into the plot of the book, and incidental to the feud, the tradition of ballad-making on local topics.

> Come all young men and maidens fair
> And hear a tale of trouble.
> Take warning, boys, shun packing guns,
> And likewise liquor's bubble.

Amy, Virginia, and Isabel cross Troublesome Creek to visit Uncle Ephraim. Isabel notices the old muzzle-loading rifle and a "strange" musical instrument hanging over his fireboard. She inquires.

" 'Dulcimores,' " he said, "used to be the onliest music in this country; the knowledge how to make 'em and pick on 'em was fotched in by our forebears. But banjos and fiddles has nigh run 'em out now."

The ancient art and industry of moonshining occurs as naturally as weeding the garden. Responding to an inquiry about the threat of typhoid up on Noah's Run, a woman remarks,

"Everybody on the branch is a-trying to stave hit off by dosting up on corn-liquor. A dram all around is what me and my man and all our young-uns takes of a morning and of a night."

To their suggestion that drinking water be boiled and flies be kept away from food, she was impervious. "Corn-liquor's the shortest way," she said.

The Quare Women is a Kentucky novel, which draws, as the author states, from early connection with Hindman Settlement School in Knott County. It is a sentimental piece of local color, an excellent example of popular literature which derives much of its appeal from its author's intimate knowledge of the folk traditions of her setting.

In hundreds of books with Kentucky locale every aspect of Kentucky history and folklore receives literary reinforcement. For a sharply contrasting use of traditional life one can turn to the short story "Old Red" by Caroline Gordon. Her locale is western Kentucky; her people are educated and professional; their language, though regional, approaches much closer to "general American." The central character is a well educated elderly man whose family deplores his intransigent independence about what other people think. His passion is fishing, the sport to which he has been confined since he became too old to hunt.

Caroline Gordon's local color items are unobtrusive but deftly effective. "He helped himself to a generous slice of batter bread. . . ." When Mr. Maury's relatives inquire about his idleness: "Well, ma'am, you know I'm a man that always likes to be learning something. Now this year I learned how to smell out fish." He goes on to tell an improbable tale about learning to smell out good fishing spots from an old Negro woman.

When Mr. Maury wants to con some Negro children into digging some fishing worms he adopts the regional pose of paternal condescension.

"D'you ever see a white man that could conjure?" he asked.

The oldest boy laid the brick he was fashioning out of mud down on a plank. He ran the tip of his tongue over his lower lip to moisten it before he spoke. "Naw, suh."

"I'm the man," Mister Maury told him. "You chillun better quit that playin' and dig me some worms."

Later, he walks along the bank humming an old ballad, "Bangum's gone to the wild boar's den." And still later, in his waking dream about the fox hunt, as the hounds are turned loose on Old Red's trail, "Old Mag knew the trick. She had stopped to give tongue by that rock."

Caroline Gordon's is a sophisticated modern short story carrying a full freight of symbol and commentary on values. The vehicle that carries the plot is a web of beliefs, attitudes, and values brought into play by common pastimes of fishing and hunting. These unobtrusively give verisimilitude and continuity so that the second element, an internal monologue, can move within a framework of surface activity. The bits of folklore are purely functional.

Furman's novel and Gordon's short story are far apart in time, geography, and style. The works of other Kentucky authors tend to fall between these extremes. Lawrence S. Thompson, in his "Folklore in the Kentucky Novel" (*Midwest Folklore*, 1953), briefly presents some of the highlights. The legend of the lost Swift silver mine, he points out, occurs in Kidwell's *The Silver Fleece*, Barton's *Pine Knot*, Powers's *In the Shadow of the Cumberlands*, and Hoppenstedt's *Secret of the Stygian River*. The Hatfield-McCoy war, he reports, has inspired three novels. Among other aspects of Kentucky history that have become legendary and have provided material for writers are Morgan's Raiders, Nancy Hanks, Indian battles and captivity, and old-time river life.

Alfred Leland Crabb's *Peace at Bowling Green* (1955), though sometimes pedestrian as a novel, is richly historical, both in terms of the events of the period leading up to the Civil War and in terms of the folkways of the time (1803–1865). Sugar trees, sorghum-making, country hams, and turnip greens begin a list of folkways from the gastronomic point of view. Crabb's careful attention to such detail suggests that he placed much value on custom as well as on historical events.

"Mister, how about some dried sasserfrus root? Makes the best tea in the world. Healthiest drink they is. Keeps down chills, toothache, and fatal diseases. I dried it last spring, and it's better now than it was the day I dug it up."

Skiles remembered what Bill Willie had told him of the virtues of sassafras tea. He bought half the man had. . . .

"Thanky, sir. Ifn I have any left I'll be back next County Court day."

Crabb describes the origin of County Court day at Bowling Green. The squires met on fourth Monday, a good time to have a horse race, shooting matches, fiddling, and general trading. Once established, the trading day assumes some aspects of local festival, a time for entertainment and gossip. Crabb works County Court day in as a recurring event or allusion thereafter, thus making use of a custom that has persisted through the years.

The use of folklore in fiction may range from merely transcriptive use of legend, song texts, and dialect (for strong local color or novelty impact) to a transformed and subtle leitmotif in works having more universal qualities.

Use of dialect presents a tricky problem for any writer. If an author is a native user of the speech, it may come naturally enough; otherwise, accurate rendition requires a good ear and careful attention. Even the native speaker may fall into the trap of overdoing distracting speech elements at the expense of the narrative. Public taste has affected the degree to which extreme dialect rendition is acceptable. Nineteenth-century humorists affected grossly distorted "eye" dialect which created some comic effects by curious misspelling. Reader acceptance of this has fallen practically to zero. Modern writers tend to use the colorful phrase or the regional word, correctly spelled, only sparingly to suggest or hint rather than to transcribe fully.

Harriette Arnow's *Mountain Path* (1936), like her later books, is a veritable catalog of folkways in Kentucky. It was written long enough ago to contain some of the excesses of dialect rendition. A fairly short passage has the following: tu (to), frum (from), ez (as), cud (could), wuz (was), uv (of). Unfortunately, those spelling oddities do practically nothing in the way of authentic rendition of regional speech. They do, however, impede reading and give the whole novel a premature patina of antiquity. Dozens of otherwise good Kentucky books gather more dust than they should on library shelves, victims of dialectal indiscretion.

Jesse Stuart is one Kentucky writer whose development over the years reflects his awareness of this change in reading tastes. He is such a prolific writer of poems, essays, short stories, and novels that the 116-page portion of a published bibliography devoted to his original writings, translations, anthologies, and adaptations (*Jesse and Jane Stuart: A Bibliography,* by Hensley C. Woodbridge, 1969) was out of date before it appeared. Stuart's use of Kentucky folklore comes as naturally to him as breathing W-Hollow air. He resides in the same hilly terrain he knew as a tenant farmer's son. When he is not on a lecture tour or off autographing a new book, he is there, watching the seasonal changes in his beloved hills and meadows and talking good plain talk with neighbors and members of his extended family. A careful study of his use of regional speech shows it to be authentic. Interestingly, some reviewers have been critical because his language rendition seems inconsistent. It is, and it should be; speakers of a regional dialect are not consistent. Stuart himself shifts easily and unconsciously from the earthy speech of the hill man to the speech of a cosmopolitan man of letters to suit the occasion.

Stuart's fiction displays a range of character and situation which permits every conceivable kind of Kentucky folklore to be used. His singing, fiddling, and dancing situations create opportunities to incorporate country dance calls and old ballads.

Uncle Op Akers, a character drawn from life (Stuart uses his real name), is a "yarb" doctor and raconteur. Uncle Op tells tall tales, one of which is about a fish he caught in the river—so big it had a sixteen-pound pike in its stomach. He tells of ghostly riders in the night, a supernatural manifestation arising from the Civil War activities of Morgan's Raiders. His knocking spirit is the ghost of a murdered Indian in a tale which incorporates a legend of lost treasure. The haunted Peddler's Well is associated with an old legend about a murdered peddler whose body was thrown down a well.

A character in *Foretaste of Glory* recounts the old "obstacle flight" story of a woman pursued by a panther as she returns home from the store. She manages to delay the panther's pursuit by tossing back packages one by one. *Head O' W-Hollow* contains a hunting tale about a "blue-tick" hound so devoted to the chase that it hung on to the fox's tail for eight days while it was being rescued from a rock crevice.

Stuart's fiction contains both the truly traditional narratives (such as the pursuing panther) and tales of his own fabrication in the folk manner. It is a tribute to his grasp of the genre that the folklorist finds himself checking index and archive to attempt to discover which is which. Stuart's use of folk materials may be largely anecdotal and transcriptive, as illustrated in the yarns of Uncle Op Akers (*The Good Spirit of Laurel Ridge*), or it may be more diffusely woven into a unified novel such as *Taps for Private Tussie*. In the latter, Grandpa Tussie is a talented narrator of tall tales, but the folklife content is really everywhere—in the speech, recreation, attitudes, and domestic activities of the Tussie family. In a sense, *Taps* is a long prose-poem in celebration of life close to nature, suggestive of the Herderian thesis that a nation's literature springs from its folk roots. The novel is also comic, but the comedy serves for more than a bellylaugh at the crudities of the improvident Tussies.

It is clearly satirical, reflecting the author's attitude toward the welfare syndrome in contemporary Appalachia.

The observation that literature (including oral literature) is an imitation of life, and that life is an imitation of literature, is nowhere better illustrated than in the "Kentucky Tragedy." The Beauchamp-Sharp affair centered around the murder of Colonel Solomon P. Sharp in 1825. The sensational and controversial trial, attempted double suicide, and execution following Beauchamp's conviction created a legend, a folk ballad, and a body of literature which includes plays, novels, articles, and historical analyses. The definitive treatment is J. Winston Coleman's *The Beauchamp-Sharp Tragedy* (1950). In this as in many of his other works "Squire" Coleman, a distinguished antiquarian and historian, puts the student in his debt for his sensitivity to Kentucky traditions. (An interesting footnote for the folklorist is the fact that Jereboam Beauchamp's family produced a distinguished contemporary scholar, Stith Thompson, the native Kentuckian at Indiana University who trained so many of the folklorists involved in Kentucky materials.)

The actions of Ann Cook and her young husband, Jereboam Beauchamp, were apparently conditioned by romantic literature of the kind that depends heavily on folk motifs. The self-image of Ann Cook is interestingly revealed in her letters, and young Beauchamp's self-image comes through in his autobiography. Though counterclaims and vindication seem to obscure the trial (highly charged with Kentucky politics), the folk attitudes toward revenge, duels, and lovers faithful even to the grave are everywhere apparent. Some of the scenes seem like reenactments of old tragic ballads. The picture of two lovers buried in each other's arms, for example, is one of the better-known ballad commonplaces:

> *Lady Margaret died of pure, pure love,*
> *Sweet William died of sorrow;*
> *They are buried in one burying ground,*
> *Both side and side together.*
>
> *Out of her grave grew a red rose,*
> *And out of his a briar;*
> *They grew in a twining true-lover's knot,*
> *The red rose and the green briar.*

The Beauchamp-Sharp affair has attracted all kinds of authors, including the folk bard. "Colonel Sharpe" is a couplet-rhyming review of the event in fifteen stanzas:

> *Gentlemen and Ladies, I pray you lend an ear;*
> *A very sad story you now shall quickly hear;*
> *It was of a bold young lawyer lived in Kentucky state*
> *Who on his own true lovyer* [sic] *with patience he did wait.*
>
> *She told him she would marry him if he would avenge her*
> *   heart*
> *Of injury had been done her by one said Colonel Sharpe,*
> *She said he had seduced her and brought her spirits low*
> *"And without some satisfaction no pleasures can I know."*
>   . . . .
> *Perhaps there's some one here who'd wish to know their*
> *   names.*
> *It was Andy Bowens Beecher and Andy Cooker's dame.*
> *And wasn't it surprising that they behaved so brave,*
> *And in each other's bosom lay mouldering in the grave?*
> *Was ever a transaction that caused so much blood*
> *Was ever a true-hearted man more constant to his love?*

Edgar Allan Poe tried a dramatic rendition of this tragedy, and William Gilmore Simms developed it into fiction: *Beauchampe* (1842) and *Charlemonte* (1856). Whereas Simms stayed fairly close to the historical event, a contemporary Kentucky author, Robert Penn Warren, departs from it to suit the artistic need of a more creative effort (*World Enough and Time*, 1950). Examination of the event and what has emerged from it makes it clear that a complex interaction of folklore, literature, and life has occurred—the folklore feeding romantic literature, and the literature providing models for behavior.

An example of such an interaction that becomes subtle and diffuse in a sophisticated modern selection is Robert Penn Warren's "Ballad of Billie Potts." In his own note to this long poem Warren states that he learned the story as a child from an old lady in Kentucky and later associated it with the legends of the outlaws of Cave-In-Rock on the Ohio River. Albert Friedman, writing in *The Ballad Revival*, associates the narrative with a ballad repeatedly reported in Kentucky, "Young Edwin in the Lowlands," a song about a murderous innkeeper who slays a young guest for his gold, only to discover later that the victim was his daughter's lover, his son-in-law to be.

> *Young Edward rose and went to bed;*
> *Had scarcely gone to sleep,*
> *When Mary's cruel father bold*
> *Into his room did creep.*
>
> *He killed him there and dragged him*
> *Down the seaside shore;*
> *He sent his body bleeding*
> *Down to the Lowland Low.*
>
> *Sweet Mary she lay sleeping,*
> *She dreamed a frightful dream*
> *She dreamed she saw her lover's blood*
> *Flowing in a stream.*
>
> *She rose, put on her clothes,*
> *Just at the break of day;*
> *"Father, where is that young man*
> *Who came last night to stay?"*
>
> *"He's dead, he's dead, no tales to tell;*
> *His gold will make a show."*
> *"You've killed the one that loved me,*
> *The one that loved me so."*

Warren's treatment of this theme in his poem is original, but it combines elements of Kentucky folklore, some of which he acquired through oral retelling. His prosody, as Friedman points out, is a combination of the form of the traditional ballad stanza and the more recent "talking-blues" or "talking-union" beat. In both content and form, then, "The Ballad of Billie Potts" is a highly original piece of modern literature tracing back to the oral literature of its author's home state. It borrows from the legendary pirates of Cave-In-Rock and the ballad about the murderous innkeeper. The ballad, in turn, centers on the motif of the mistaken murder of kin, a motif which belongs to world literature, surfacing in such disparate works as *Sohrab and Rustum* and *Oedipus Rex*. Warren brings it to life again in a setting he calls "the land between the rivers" in Kentucky.

Folk literature, like honeysuckle on a hillside, rooted deeply in the fertile loam of common humanity, branches out in a tangle of tendrils and bloom. Kentucky is a good host to both honeysuckle and folklore.

8

SUMMING UP

KENTUCKY of the 1970s offers many opportunities for folkloristic inquiry. After two centuries of growth and change the image of Kentucky is vastly more complicated than it was when eager pioneers settled the virgin land. Intertwining strands of imported and home-grown expressions combine to produce an idiom of the people that is always both old and new, always a unique blend in its time and place. Collection and study continue to bear fruit.

When Herbert Halpert left Murray in the 1950s, he shared his field-collected materials with the growing Western Kentucky Collection at Bowling Green. D. K. Wilgus kept adding to it until he departed for the University of California at Los Angeles in 1962. In the meantime, George Boswell continued to send his students to informants in the vicinity of Morehead, and William Hugh Jansen continued to give his attention to the Lexington area. With the departure of Wilgus, the *Kentucky Folklore Record* moved its headquarters to Murray and the editorship of Hensley C. Woodbridge.

When Stith Thompson retired at Indiana University, his post was filled by Richard Dorson, another Harvard-trained folktale specialist. One of Dorson's early students was Lynwood Montell, Kentucky native son whose graduate studies were to produce *The Saga of*

Coe Ridge. After completing his Hoosier pilgrimage, Montell returned to Campbellsville College, where he began an intensive program of field collection.

In the meantime, Kenneth and Mary Clarke moved from Indiana University's southeastern campus at Jeffersonville to Bowling Green and brought the *Kentucky Folklore Record* back to its birthplace at Western. Woodbridge, like some other early supporters, was leaving the state. George Boswell at Morehead, then president of the Kentucky Folklore Society, assisted in the transition. Kenneth Clarke was one of Stith Thompson's students. Mary Clarke had done extensive field collecting in eastern Kentucky and West Virginia, some of which she used in her study of Jesse Stuart (*Jesse Stuart's Kentucky,* 1968).

With the encouragement and support of Gordon Wilson, then living in retirement and continuing his study of the Mammoth Cave region, the Clarkes set out to expand the folklore curriculum at Western—traditionally the stronghold of such studies in Kentucky. With the expansion of course offerings came the need for help, and help came in the person of Lynwood Montell, who moved to Western. Additional part-time help also became available when Jean Thomason completed her master's thesis at Western with more strength in folklore than had been previously available.

As courses continued to expand and as an undergraduate minor in folk studies developed, still more help was needed. The Clarkes turned the *Kentucky Folklore Record* over to the able editorship of Charles Guthrie, a Burkesville native on the English faculty at Western. Guthrie had studied with Jansen at the University of Kentucky.

Finally, with the energetic guidance of Montell, a graduate degree program (Master of Arts in Folk Studies) developed at Western. Camilla Collins joined the faculty to meet the need for additional instruction. She had pursued her graduate studies at Indiana University under the direction of Richard Dorson.

The first master's thesis to be completed in the graduate folk studies program at Western was "The Little People of Pea Ridge," by David Sutherland in 1973. Sutherland combined his skill in photography with his course work to produce an unusual study of the traditional activities in a single small community.

Expansion of course offerings, enrollment, and faculty was matched by the expansion of the Western Kentucky University Collection of Folklore and Folklife. Now fully integrated with the other library services, it contains the Gordon Wilson collection, copies of portions of the Wilgus collection, the Halpert collection, the Boswell collection, and the Montell collection. It also contains clusters of other specialty material such as copies of Sharon Huizinga's "word-wagon" tapes from her Kentucky collection for the *Dictionary of American Regional English*. The whole complex is, then, a major research facility for students of Kentucky folkways and for students of folkways outside of Kentucky who wish to do comparative research.

Because the only major work on Kentucky folk beliefs (Thomas and Thomas, *Kentucky Superstitions*) is more than a half-century old, a new project on this subject is taking form. This involves the pooling of efforts and materials by Wilgus in California, Montell at Western, and Leonard Roberts at Pikeville. The wider base of operations is also indicated by recently developed oral history projects at Alice Lloyd College and at the University of Louisville.

Some readers may have wondered at our failure to mention persons, institutions, and publications that they have associated with Kentucky folklore. Berea College, for example, has never given academic recognition to the study of regional folklore as such. The college does offer an undergraduate major in Appalachian studies under the direction of Loyal Jones. By the intent of its founders and its present leaders, Berea attempts to bring to the region's youth a high quality education that transcends regionalism. To expect extensive folklore activities of a scholarly nature at Berea is to mistake the institution's role in mountain culture. Berea's folk dancers are well trained performers of dances from many eras and many lands. Berea's weavers and other craftsmen are highly trained, producing revival items of considerable aesthetic appeal. Here, as in many of Kentucky's nonacademic folk festivals and crafts fairs, a happy blend of traditional and modern elements appeals to popular taste, and sometimes achieves the level of art.

Diverse activities relating to or peripheral to folklore at Lees College, Pikeville College, and several of the Kentucky community colleges, among other institutions, are adding to the awareness Kentuckians have always had of their rich heritage from oral tradition.

The publication of *Mountain Life and Work* by the Council of the Southern Mountains, closely associated with Berea, has often included materials of interest to folklorists, although folklore has never been a principal focus.

Our account of the harvest of Kentucky's oral traditions has been limited by the interests of Kentucky folklorists in the past. Other ripe fields of folklore study await a new generation of reapers, whose interests may focus on oral traditions of the Negro, the Bluegrass, or the tradition-oriented displaced minorities in Kentucky cities rather than on the Anglo-American song and story of the Kentucky highlands. Increased attention to such virgin territory for collection, analysis, and interpretation may gradually overcome the present imbalance which stresses Child ballads and European *Märchen,* which, for all their significance, have never dominated the Kentucky folk scene.

Today it is technically possible and academically desirable to snatch from oblivion, accurately and sensitively, the verbal and musical arts, the material culture, and the unrecorded history of those formerly nameless and faceless generations of people who have altered the landscape of Kentucky with their hands and who have created the image of Kentucky with their expressions—the folk.

Published Sources

Anderson, John Q. *With the Bark On: Popular Humor of the Old South.* Nashville, Tenn.: Vanderbilt University Press, 1967.

Arnow, Harriette Simpson. *Mountain Path.* New York: Convici Friede Publishers, 1936.

Campbell, Marie. *Tales from the Cloud Walking Country.* Bloomington: Indiana University Press, 1958.

Clark, Thomas D. *The Kentucky.* Revised edition. Lexington, Ky.: Henry Clay Press, 1969.

Clarke, Kenneth. *Uncle Bud Long: Birth of a Kentucky Folk Legend.* Lexington: University Press of Kentucky, 1973.

Clarke, Mary Washington. *Jesse Stuart's Kentucky.* New York: McGraw-Hill Book Co., 1968.

Cohen, Anne B. *Poor Pearl, Poor Girl.* Austin: University of Texas Press, 1973.

Coleman, J. Winston, Jr. *The Beauchamp-Sharp Tragedy.* Frankfort, Ky.: Roberts Printing Co., 1950.

Combs, Josiah H. *All That's Kentucky: An Anthology.* Louisville: John P. Morton and Co., 1915.

———— *Folk-Songs of the Southern United States.* Edited by D. K. Wilgus. Austin: University of Texas Press, 1967.

Crabb, Alfred Leland. *Peace at Bowling Green.* Indianapolis: Bobbs-Merrill Co., 1955.

Dorson, Richard M. *American Negro Folktales.* New York: Fawcett World Library, 1967.

Emrich, Duncan. *Folklore on the American Land.* Boston: Little, Brown and Co., 1972.

Field, Thomas P. *A Guide to Kentucky Place Names.* Kentucky Geological Survey, Series X. Lexington: University of Kentucky, 1961.

Friedman, Albert B. *The Ballad Revival.* Chicago: University of Chicago Press, 1961.

Furman, Lucy. *The Quare Women.* Boston: Atlantic Monthly Press, 1923.

Gordon, Caroline. *Old Red and Other Stories.* New York: Cooper Square Publishers, 1971.

Greenway, John. *American Folksongs of Protest.* Philadelphia: University of Pennsylvania Press, 1953.

Guthrie, Charles S. *Riddles from the Cumberland Valley.* Bowling Green, Ky.: Kentucky Folklore Society, 1973.

Karpeles, Maud. *Cecil Sharp: His Life and Work.* Chicago: University of Chicago Press, 1967.

Montell, William Lynwood. *The Saga of Coe Ridge.* Knoxville: University of Tennessee Press, 1970.

Moore, Arthur K. *The Frontier Mind: A Cultural Analysis of the Kentucky Frontiersman.* Lexington: University of Kentucky Press, 1957.

Niles, John Jacob. *The Ballad Book of John Jacob Niles.* Boston: Houghton Mifflin Co., 1961.

Ritchie, Jean. *Singing Family of the Cumberlands.* New York: Oxford University Press, 1955.

Roberts, Leonard. *Old Greasybeard: Tales from the Cumberland Gap.* Detroit: Folklore Associates, 1969.

———— *South from Hell-fer-Sartin: Kentucky Mountain Folktales.* Lexington: University of Kentucky Press, 1955.

Rourke, Constance M. *American Humor: A Study of the National Character.* New York: Harcourt, Brace and Co., 1931.

Sharp, Cecil J. *English Folk-Songs from the Southern Appalachians.* Edited by Maud Karpeles, 2 vols. London: Oxford University Press, 1932.

Still, James. *Way Down Yonder on Troublesome Creek: Appalachian Riddles & Rusties.* New York: G. P. Putnam's Sons, 1974.

Stuart, Jesse. *Taps for Private Tussie.* New York: E. P. Dutton and Co., 1943.

———— *The Good Spirit of Laurel Ridge.* New York: McGraw-Hill Book Co., 1953.

Thomas, Daniel, and Thomas, Lucy. *Kentucky Superstitions.* Princeton, N.J.: Princeton University Press, 1920.

Thomas, Jean. *Ballad Makin' in the Mountains of Kentucky.* New York: Henry Holt Co., 1939.

Thompson, Lawrence S. *Kentucky Tradition.* Hamden, Conn.: Shoe String Press, 1956.

Townsend, William H. *Hundred Proof: Salt River Sketches*

and Memoirs of the Bluegrass. Lexington: University of Kentucky Press, 1964.

Warren, Robert Penn. *World Enough and Time.* New York: Random House, 1950.

Wells, Evelyn K. *The Ballad Tree.* New York: Ronald Press Co., 1950.

Wilgus, D. K. *Anglo-American Folksong Scholarship since 1898.* New Brunswick, N.J.: Rutgers University Press, 1959.

Wilson, Gordon, Sr. *Folklore of the Mammoth Cave Region.* Edited by Lawrence S. Thompson. Bowling Green, Ky.: Kentucky Folklore Society, 1968.

Woodbridge, Hensley C. *Jesse and Jane Stuart: A Bibliography.* Murray, Ky.: Murray State University, 1969.

Unpublished Sources

The narratives which are not credited to the *Kentucky Folklore Record* or to other published sources are from the Western Kentucky University Folklore and Folklife Collection or from the authors' manuscript collection of Kentucky folktales. The tale about the duck hunter at Horse Cave is a summary rather than a verbatim transcription of a tape recording. Similarly, the tales about the child with a rattlesnake companion and about the clever boy who used the deer's tongue for evidence are summaries of oral renditions. The vote-buying narrative is slightly modified to alter names and locality in deference to the informant's desire for anonymity. The Johnson County and Celina ghost tales are verbatim transcriptions from tape-recorded interviews conducted by university students. The humorous ghost tale by Earl Thomas is a transcription of his rendition in an unrehearsed story-telling session recorded on videotape for a half-hour television documentary produced at Western Kentucky University.